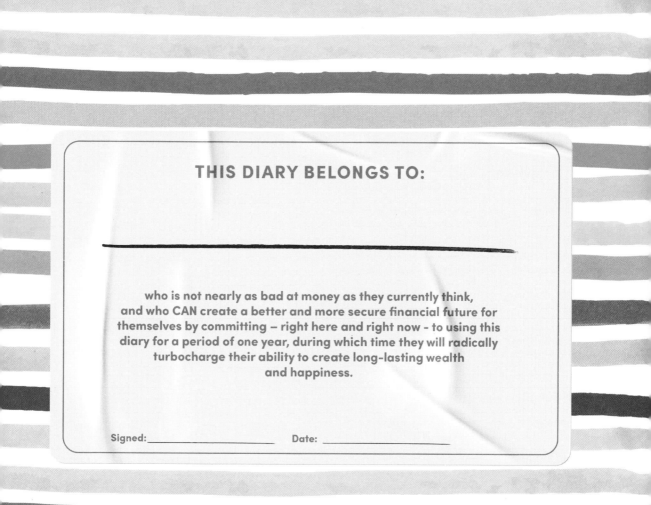

THIS DIARY BELONGS TO:

_____

who is not nearly as bad at money as they currently think,
and who CAN create a better and more secure financial future for
themselves by committing – right here and right now - to using this
diary for a period of one year, during which time they will radically
turbocharge their ability to create long-lasting wealth
and happiness.

Signed: _____ Date: _____

THE MONEY DIARY

End your money worries NOW & take control of your financial future

JESSICA IRVINE

WILEY

First published in 2024 by John Wiley & Sons Australia, Ltd
Level 4, 600 Bourke St, Melbourne Victoria 3000, Australia.

Typeset in Garamond Premier Pro 12pt/15pt

ISBN: 978-1-394-20872-2

A catalogue record for this
book is available from the
National Library of Australia

Cover and internal page design by Alissa Dinallo

Disclaimer
The material in this publication is of the nature of general comment only, and does
not represent professional advice. It is not intended to provide specific guidance for
particular circumstances and it should not be relied on as the basis for any decision
to take action or not take action on any matter which it covers. Readers should
obtain professional advice where appropriate, before making any such decision.
To the maximum extent permitted by law, the author and publisher disclaim all
responsibility and liability to any person, arising directly or indirectly from any person
taking or not taking action based on the information in this publication.

Printed in Singapore
M125920_210823

CONTENTS

WELCOME TO YOUR NEW DIARY!

Oh, hi there! It's me, Jess, a personal finance expert and the creator of your new favourite diary. You're so welcome!

It's no trouble, really. Actually, it's a bit selfish. What you're holding in your hands is the dream diary I've always wished I had had to track my own finances. It's based on the unique system I've spent years honing and developing to help me get a complete picture of my money and plan for my future with confidence.

I'm so excited to use it myself and now to share it with you to spread the word about how life-changing it can be to really take control of your money. To see it in action, follow me on Instagram (@moneywithjess) and don't forget to tag me in any posts as you embark on your exciting journey towards cultivating a better relationship with your money.

From the earliest of ages, I've always written diaries. I've kept many of them, including a spiral-bound diary from my final year of primary school. In it, I chronicle—in excruciating detail which I will spare you—my passionate and completely unrequited 'first love' for a certain honeycomb-haired classmate who, for privacy's sake, we shall refer to only as 'C'.

But time moves on, and by year's end, it appears I had switched allegiance to classmate 'S': 'Oh God I love him. Although he doesn't know it. I feel he is more special to me than "C". He is always going to have a special place in my heart as my first love, along with "C".'

My outpourings of love for both 'C' and 'S' are overwhelmed, however, by my towering adoration for actor Luke Perry, aka 'Dylan' from the 1990s TV show *90210*, whose poster hung over my bed for many a formative year:

'I feel that I have a very special relationship with him,' little 12-year-old Jess confessed to the pages of her diary. 'Although I know I can never have him, that doesn't stop me from wishing. I feel that my love for him is not another crush but something special.'

What can I say? Clearly, little Jess had a lot of love to give.

And on it went, diary entries about boys punctuated only by angst-ridden meditations over who was my 'best friend' and all the usual pre-pubescent frustrations with certain family members.

Growing up, I concluded succinctly in one particular entry, 'It's a bummer'.

And I stand by that.

Why a money diary?

There's magic in diaries, I believe. They create treasured time capsules, just waiting to be unlocked and rediscovered at some later date by an older, wiser version of ourselves.

But they're also a therapeutic tool, providing immediate relief to the user. Used openly and honestly, they give us the space to vent our emotions, to explore our inner minds and to Get. It. Out. Whatever 'it' happens to be.

The simple act of getting information out of your head (or bank accounts, as we shall see) and putting it onto paper can go a very long way to helping alleviate the anxiety and stress we may feel over any topic. Of course, being able to tell a trusted friend or advisor has its place. But there's nothing like a private diary to help us park our difficult feelings and reflect on how our thoughts and actions may be contributing to any distress.

In recent years, I've applied this technique to my finances, chronicling every dollar I spend and then reflecting at the end of each month on the value it has or has not brought into my life.

The point of this book is to encourage you to give it a try it, too. Why? Not because you're infatuated with your money, like little Jess was with Luke Perry. Quite the opposite.

After two decades of writing and researching money-related topics and questions, I know love is very far from the emotion most people have towards money.

Anxiety, helplessness and overwhelm? Yes. Love? No. And if I had to pick one emotion representing the overriding human feeling towards money? It's fear. Fear of not having enough. Fear of making bad decisions. Fear, in some cases, of even looking at your money and figuring out what situation you're in.

And I get it. To some extent, a degree of fear around money is warranted—primal, even. We all need a certain level of resources at our disposal to stay alive; to put a roof over our head at night and food in our bellies.

But unchecked and excessive fear around our finances can be counterproductive. That's because the emotion of fear is known to drive a range of avoidance or escapist behaviours. You see a bear so you run.

And yet, when it comes to money, fear — coupled with a lack of financial education — can drive a range of unhelpful habits, such as mindless spending, not checking your accounts or opening bills, not setting goals, avoiding important conversations with your spouse or loved ones, or not seeking the right advice and support to make important financial decisions. It's known as the 'ostrich effect' and is just one of the many cognitive biases researchers have discovered human beings have to constantly work against to get better with their money, and which I wrote about in my previous book *Money with Jess: Your Ultimate Guide to Household Budgeting*.

This book builds on those findings while also providing the private space you need to really start delving into your own emotions, thoughts and behaviours around money. It is, of course, also a calendar that you can use to organise your life and, most importantly, to track your spending. Finally, and perhaps most importantly, it's a space to reflect on whether your current spending is in line with your highest goals and values.

My aim is to do as much as I can to help alleviate the suffering so many people feel when it comes to thinking about money.

As a single mum, I have faced my own challenges when it comes to managing my money. I have felt that sting of fear. But with time and dedication to tracking my money, I've arrived at a place of security and empowerment when it comes to managing my own money. It's called 'financial wellness' and it's not as far off as you might think.

What is financial wellness?

Go ahead and try to picture someone who you think embodies the definition of financial wellness. What do they look like, dress like and have in their lives?

If you're like most people, you'll start to conjure up images of famously rich people: actors, famous singers or business people. They drive the Tesla, own the handbags and live in the manor-style house.

Basically just anyone with a s*#t tonne of money, right?

Wrong.

Certainly, having a lot of savings at your disposal contributes very directly to higher levels of financial wellbeing. But not always. And it's not a necessary condition for someone to experience financial wellness.

Just as we have some pretty warped ideas as a society about what physically healthy people (visible washboard abs) or mentally healthy people (always happy, always smiling) *look* like, real financial health can also be harder to spot. And the good news is, it's a lot more attainable than you may think.

In recent decades there has been an ever-evolving attempt by academics to define financial health. We used to talk a lot about 'financial literacy' and the importance of building people's knowledge base around money concepts. Then, we started talking more about 'financial capability': essentially, a person's ability to actually make sound financial decisions.

The latest evolution is to talk about 'financial wellbeing', which I like—though it can run the risk of sounding a bit 'woo woo'. The distinctly non–woo woo Consumer Financial Protection Bureau in the United States defines financial wellbeing as 'A condition wherein a person can fully meet current and ongoing financial obligations, can feel secure in their financial future, and is able to make choices that allow them to enjoy life'.

More specifically, the bureau says people need to meet four criteria to be financially well:

1. Have control over day-to-day, month-to-month finances
2. Have the capacity to absorb a financial shock
3. Be on track to meet their financial goals
4. Have the financial freedom to make the choices that allow one to enjoy life.

Truthfully, there are many definitions of financial wellness flying around, but that's a pretty good start. How close do you think you are?

Complete the financial wellbeing questionnaire on the next page to gauge your current level of financial wellness.

Go on, pick up a pen and give it a try!

We'll return to this later, so having some idea of your starting point will be very useful, I promise.

FINANCIAL WELLBEING QUESTIONNAIRE

If you'd like to test your current level of financial wellbeing, researchers at Australia's The Melbourne Institute and the Commonwealth Bank designed the following simple test to help. Simply work your way through it and tick a response for each part. Don't overthink it – go with your gut.

How well do the following statements describe you or your situation?

I can enjoy life because of the way I'm managing my money

☐ Not at all   ☐ Very little   ☐ Somewhat   ☐ Very well   ☐ Completely

I could handle a major unexpected expense

☐ Not at all   ☐ Very little   ☐ Somewhat   ☐ Very well   ☐ Completely

When it comes to how you think and feel about your finances, please indicate the extent to which you agree or disagree with the following statements.

I feel on top of my day-to-day finances

☐ Disagree strongly   ☐ Disagree   ☐ Neither agree nor disagree   ☐ Agree   ☐ Agree strongly

I am comfortable with my current levels of spending relative to the funds I have coming in

☐ Disagree strongly   ☐ Disagree   ☐ Neither agree nor disagree   ☐ Agree   ☐ Agree strongly

I am on track to have enough money to provide for my financial needs in the future

☐ Disagree strongly   ☐ Disagree   ☐ Neither agree nor disagree   ☐ Agree   ☐ Agree strongly

---

Now, for each question answered, give yourself a score of between 0 and 4. Give a score of 4 for each statement you answered 'Completely' or 'Agree strongly' with, 3 for each 'Very well' or 'Agree', 2 for each 'Somewhat' or 'Neither agree nor disagree', 1 for each 'Very little' or 'Disagree' and 0 for each 'Not at all' or 'Disagree strongly'.

Add up your total score and multiply it by 5 to get a score out of 100.

MY SCORE: _____

After completing this questionnaire, compare your result to those of a survey of 4000 Australians conducted in 2017. Respondents scored a median of 55 points out of 100. Here's the full breakdown:

Score	Category	% of respondents
77.5 to 100	'Doing great'	9.0
50 to 75	'Getting by'	52.7
25 to 47.5	'Just coping'	29.4
0 to 22.5	'Having trouble'	8.9

So, how did you do?

Interestingly, these self-reported scores for financial wellness were found to be highly correlated with other independent measures of respondents' actual savings levels and behaviours. In essence, when people are struggling, they know it. Trust your instincts.

Please do not be downhearted if you are less than impressed with your own score.

Whether it's learning to better manage your day-to-day bills with more confidence, saving extra for emergencies, working towards financial goals or honing your ability to make good decisions on how to spend your money, I believe progress towards improved financial wellness is possible for everyone, no matter your starting point.

That's what this whole book is about. I got you. Just keep reading.

To really kick things off, I think it's important we take a step back and get our stories straight on what money really *is*.

What is money, anyway?

I know we're all busy, so let me cut to the chase.

Money is, at its heart, a means of exchange and a store of value. As a worker, you give up your valuable time and skillset to receive money. You then use that money to buy all the things you need and want to live the best life possible.

Earning money involves sacrifice of both your freedom and pieces of your precious and finite lifespan. But in return, it provides the opportunity to enjoy wonderful things such as shelter, food, hot water, books and holidays.

Viewed this way, the money you acquire is, in a very real sense, a measure of the value of your time and life. Therefore, how you spend your money is quite literally how you spend your life: the precious minutes, hours and days you had to give up to earn it. Should you be so careless with your life units? That's up to you. But once you see money this way, I think it's harder to be so frivolous.

Now, the entire endgame of this exchange process is to acquire enough income to buy all the goods and services you will need and want throughout your lifetime. Because while it might seem far off to some (closer to others), at some point you will be unable or unwilling to work. So some degree of saving during your working lifetime is necessary to fund your retirement consumption needs and wants. To be financially successful, then, you need to spend less than you earn during your working life and save and invest the difference so it can be drawn-down in retirement—that golden age when you get to blow it all on cocktails and flashy campervans (woo hoo!) or, you know, hip replacements, depending on how things go…

That's it. That's all you need to know about money. Spend less than you earn; invest the rest. Rinse and repeat.

It's a startlingly simple idea in theory, but one that very few people seem to grasp. Or, if they do, many people have an inordinately hard time implementing it.

Which is actually not so surprising when you look at the world we live in and the broad sweep of human history. In short: there was a time when our ancestors spent most of their time scrambling around searching for food. Today, we can have a tub of Ben & Jerry's delivered straight to our mouth holes with a few mere taps of a smartphone screen.

Better yet, there is no shortage of consumer-debt companies willing to let us bypass the whole 'work to earn money to pay for stuff' thing. Instead, they'll let you buy something now and promise to pay it back later (and whack you with severe penalties if you don't).

We spend our lives viewing the social media accounts of beautiful people, eating beautiful food, dressed in beautiful clothes in beautiful holiday destinations. And it makes us feel bad so we whip open our web browsers and order up some quick fix of consumption—whether it's new shoes, a handbag or the latest gadget—to make us feel better.

We live in a world of almost infinite temptations to spend, and no shortage of companies willing to indulge us in our overspending ways. Until, of course, we're drowning in debt and our credit rating is shot.

And look, if you had to pick a problem — between scratching around for food or being stuck in a cycle of perpetual overspending, debt, stress and overwork — I guess our current problem is the one to have.

But it's not a pain-free lifestyle. Money stress is real and it can come for anyone — rich or poor — who fails to take control of their financial life and spending.

Even if you don't end up in debt, you can end up working a lot harder and a lot longer than necessary to fund your endless desire for more 'stuff'.

I know everyone is hoping to find the next get-rich scheme or investment with astronomical returns to bypass the boring business of working hard, saving and keeping their spending in check.

And I know some personal-finance gurus think it's better to encourage you to focus all your energies on boosting your income. I agree to the extent that ensuring you are getting paid fairly for your skills is always a good idea.

But I also firmly believe that if you fail to ever get a handle on your spending habits, you will never be financially secure, no matter your income. Money will continue to slip through your fingers like sand if you don't have a *process* in place to manage it.

Because here's one thing I've learned about money: it's much easier to spend it than it is to earn it.

Much like a hard workout can be offset by the consumption of one delicious piece of cake, it's easy — easier, in fact — to spend an entire day's, week's, or even month's wage with the click of a few buttons.

It's not your fault; it's the way the world works. But if you want to be financially well in this world, you do need to fight against its inbuilt tendencies.

And that can be hard. I know when I'm stressed or time poor, I tend to spend more on conveniences such as takeout food and online purchases (my weakness is books!). But I'm also here to tell you that you can slow down, take some deep breaths and reflect on the way you are choosing to spend your hard-earned money.

Since I've been tracking my money and reflecting on my purchases using the system in this book, I have definitely had success curbing my overspending ways. This has allowed me to save and invest more, which has in turn given me greater financial security and peace.

Just as importantly, when I do spend money, I have a better sense of whether the purchases I'm making align with my personal values and truly bring me joy. I've honed my radar for joyful spending. And that's the real win.

So, how are we going to get you there? Let me explain.

How to boost your financial wellbeing

Obviously, by winning a million dollars! Failing that, buying this book was a pretty good start.

Part one of this book is dedicated to getting you in the right mindset to make the changes needed to get you in the driver's seat of your day-to-day money decision making.

You will learn to identify and label your emotions. You'll then learn how to identify your underlying money beliefs and thoughts, along with strategies for choosing new and more helpful thoughts.

We will work through exercises to help you hone your sense of what activities bring you joy and what values you want to live by.

We'll take a money 'before' snapshot, to see where you are currently at with your moolah, before setting some modest goals for where you want to go.

In part two, I'll help you move from contemplation to action by teaching you how to follow the money management system I use for my own day-to-day finances. There's no elaborate system of bank accounts—just good old-fashioned pen and paper (and colourful highlighters!) to help you track your incomings and outgoings and make sure you're in surplus.

You'll find a calendar marked with months, but no specific dates, so you can begin working in any month and in any year. Each month, there will be money-saving exercises and strategies to keep you motivated. We'll set intentions at the start of each month, and review progress and outcomes at the end.

I'll be with you every step of the way.

In part three, we'll take all the information you have gathered and study it. You'll arrive at an estimate of your annual expenses that you can then use to determine your emergency fund size and targets for retirement spending. This can also be presented to banks and financial institutions when you are applying for finance.

Finally, we'll look back on the year that was, and consider strategies to help you keep on the track to greater financial wellness and empowerment.

Most importantly, we'll make it fun — and colourful. If you haven't already, now's the time to go out and buy a set of 10 different-coloured highlighters that you'll use to colour code and categorise your spending throughout the year.

Colouring in your diary pages will not only help you to easily identify patterns in your spending. It's also fun. It's like colouring in for adults, and extremely soothing in some way.

There's magic in the highlighters, people. Trust me.

I firmly believe everyone should try tracking their spending for a period at least once in their life. Maybe you'll gain all the insight you need in one year. Maybe you'll enjoy the power of exerting control and knowing what surplus you have at the end of each month to throw towards your identified money goals so much that — like me — you'll just keep going each year.

Most money books start by just telling you to track your spending, before moving on to more exciting things like investing.

But I'm going to hold your hand and keep you on track to actually achieve this crucial first step. And not just for one day or one week, but an entire year, to make sure you capture many of the bigger expenses in life that only hit irregularly, like servicing your car or paying your annual home insurance bill.

I firmly believe that committing to tracking your spending will radically transform the way you think about your money and arm you with powerful insights you can use to transform your life for the better.

I've been tracking my spending like this for several years now and I know the peace and stability this simple habit can bring to the often turbulent topic of money.

I have a beef with philosophers, which you'll read about in chapter 1, but it was the philosopher Aristotle who said, 'We are what we repeatedly do. Excellence, then, is not an act, but a habit.'

We are about to embark on an adventure together, you and I, to equip you with some healthy habits around managing your money.

I encourage you to show your completed diary to your banker when you apply for a loan, your accountant when you come to do your tax, or your financial advisor to give them an immediate picture of where you're at with your money.

You're about to get all your important financial information together in one place — a complete picture of your money set-up. This will not only make you feel more in control of your money, but potentially help you to grow it faster by borrowing and investing with more confidence, possibly minimising your tax (keep your receipts!) and planning for a more comfortable retirement.

Worth a bit of time, eh?

I'm so excited for you to take this journey with me.

Let's begin.

GET READY

CHAPTER 1

UNLEASH YOUR HIDDEN SUPERPOWER TO CHOOSE YOUR LIFE

Around the age of 18, I packed up all my Luke Perry posters and childhood diaries in a big memorabilia box, parked it at my parents' house and set sail for university, where I undertook a dual major degree in Philosophy and Political Economy. I would go on to put the political economy part of that degree to good effect as an economics journalist for nearly two decades at some of Australia's most prestigious and esteemed newspapers.

The study of philosophy, however—I'm afraid to say—left me with little more than a gnawing sense of existential dread and, even more problematically, a sneaky suspicion that human beings lack the free will to do anything to consciously alter their life's course (Luke Perry had, after all, never been in contact).

You see, in my first year, I undertook a common course of study called 'The philosophy of the mind', which seeks to explore the so-called 'mind–body problem' of how objects in the physical world, like your body, relate to mental phenomena such as thoughts and consciousness. Surely, the theory goes, these categories are two separate things—matter and non-matter—and if so, what is the relationship between the two?

Most people find it easy enough to sense how physical changes in the body can produce different mental states. You touch fire, you feel pain, and so on. But what about the opposite? Can immaterial things—such as thoughts—impact the physical? Can you think your way into doing stuff?

Turns out, there's a school of philosophical thought that reckons we can't. It's called 'epiphenomenalism'. I distinctly remember encountering a picture in a textbook illustrating the idea as akin to a steam train — namely, that all our mental states and thoughts are simply the puffs of smoke arising from our physical bodies. It suggested that we are as powerless to stop or change the direction of the steam train (our bodies) as the steam arising from a train would be to stop the train in its tracks.

You are, in effect, simply observing your own life as if it were a TV show: passively and powerlessly. Free will is a myth.

Pretty dark, right?

Unfortunately, it turns out to be rather hard to win the argument against epiphenomenalism and definitively prove the existence of free will. At least, I couldn't in my first-year papers. Cue a rather dark era of me thinking I didn't have much agency, and watching rather too much TV.

I think it's actually pretty common to be a puff-of-smoke observer of your life, until you wake up one day realising the steam train of your life has taken you in a direction you're not quite happy with. You suddenly feel the need to stand up, pull the emergency chain, get off the train and head in a new direction.

At which point, you're left standing by the side of the tracks, somewhat stunned, realising you *did* have the power to choose after all—and your philosophy teacher really ought to have given you a better steer in life. But you can't really blame them—or anyone—entirely and you have to start taking responsibility for your own life and choices.

I still don't think I can write a definitive philosophical treatise to prove why free will exists. I just know that life is better when you believe it does.

Perhaps things would have gone differently for me if instead of studying philosophy, I'd chosen a major in psychology. Turns out psychologists are pretty on board with the idea that human beings are able to change their lives for the better—it's sort of their whole jam.

In particular, the fields of cognitive behavioural therapy and dialectical behaviour therapy have evolved to help equip human beings with the mental tools to identify our emotional states and the underlying thoughts. This enables us to try to shape and modify behaviours, both to promote healthy ones, like walking more, and to try to eliminate harmful ones, like smoking.

Indeed, in the field of health behaviours there has been much work done on what it takes to make people change and adopt healthier ways of life.

The Stages of Change model

In the 1970s, two researchers, Prochaska and DiClemente, developed the Stages of Change model to describe six distinct stages that can be observed in patients who successfully quit smoking.

They found change tended to happen via a cyclical process comprising roughly six stages, as shown here.

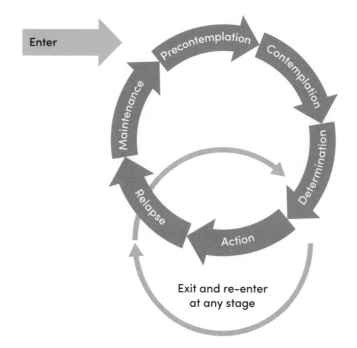

Precontemplation

A person in the stage of precontemplation has no discernible desire to change their behaviour. They either don't see the problem or lack the desire to make any changes.

When it comes to behaviours to do with their money, some people, of course, might register in this stage because they're actually really happy with their situation. They have a money management system that works for them and they are reliably saving for their certain future. If that's you, then great! (And also, sorry! Perhaps you might know someone else who needs help? If so, please do pass this book on.)

However, many people in precontemplation about changing their money behaviours are, in fact, people who are stuck. Yes, they feel a bit stressed about money. But they don't believe they have any power to change. In fact, they often blame others — society, friends or spouses — for their financial difficulties. They simply don't see their role in their financial problems, or, if they do, they see no way to change. Their money problems are just an epiphenomenon dangling over their heads like a puff of steam above a train.

It sucks to be stuck in precontemplation.

Contemplation

Chances are, though, if you're holding this diary and have read this far, you have made it to the contemplation stage. And if so, well done. This is perhaps one of the most crucial leaps you will make. You are aware that money causes some suffering in your life, and you are interested in changing.

You haven't actually decided to change, mind you. Oh no. Yes, you want more money and security, but you also really love your current lifestyle, which might include buying lots of new shoes or going out regularly.

In the contemplation stage of change, you spend a lot of time weighing up the various pros and cons of changing your behaviour. Sure, committing to tracking your spending might bring you more peace of mind and visibility around your money, but what if you didn't like what you saw? What if it meant giving up buying those things you love?

If you're in that pros-versus-cons state of mind, let me put your mind at ease. I'm not actually going to ask you to spend less. This diary is simply about observing your spending and resulting surplus and shortfall each month. If you track your spending and happen to discover that you are comfortably in surplus each month, and *love* and value every purchase you make, then yippee — you can keep doing it! Engaging in the process will still have brought you valuable information on your monthly and annual spending, which will help you to borrow and invest with confidence.

Maybe, just maybe, however, your tracking will lead you to realise that you are spending too much on some things and you do want to make some changes. You get to choose to do that, too. All this diary — and committing to tracking and reviewing your spending—really gives you is visibility around your current behaviours. It's up to you entirely if you want to change any of them.

If I'm being honest, the main 'con' involved in my approach to money management—the one thing you will have to invest in if you choose to proceed with me—is a bit of time and effort writing down and reviewing your spending. On the 'pro' side, I think it's possible to come to enjoy this process. Like writing in an actual diary or doing something repetitive, like gardening or colouring in, it can become a mindful process.

But it does take time and effort—and more so at the start. So if you're still in the contemplation phase of wanting to change your behaviour when it comes to money and adopt my strategy of tracking your money, there you have it. That's the trade-off: you'll need to find some time to do it, possibly deducted from—I don't know—scrolling your phone, watching Netflix or complaining to your friends about how broke you are.

All I'm saying is that there are ways to make time for things that matter. And finding a path to financial security and peace of mind matters—quite a lot.

Determination

Perhaps you're internally screaming at me by this point: 'Yes! Yes Jess, I am ready for change! Stop labouring all this philosophical and psychological mumbo jumbo and let's start!'

Great. Bottle that.

You're going to need it for when times get tough and you start to think that the actual process of tracking and looking at money is really boring, which I assure you, *will* happen at some point while using this diary.

That's why I have dedicated part one of this book to really getting you into the right headspace for change, before we use part two of the book to hit the all-important fourth stage of the model of change.

Action

Lights, camera, action! People in this stage of change are actually doing it—they're changing. They've committed to taking action and are implementing a changed behaviour in their lives. It could be quitting smoking, or changing how they exercise or eat. For you, it's taking action to monitor and reflect on your spending using this diary.

You're in your first month of tracking and you're going strong. You love colour coding your spending with highlighters. You're telling your friends about this cool new thing you're doing.

And then *bam!*

Relapse

Your boss calls you to work an extra shift. It's school holidays and the kids are climbing the walls. You have a health scare. Days go by. Then weeks. You haven't updated your spending tracker and you're convinced you're a failure.

Because that's the thing about change. It's actually pretty common for people committing to a certain behavioural change—like tracking their spending—to relapse and fall back to the earlier stages of change, before giving it another crack.

This is an entirely natural and to-be-expected stage of change, as the theory goes. The good news is that getting yourself out of precontemplation was actually the hardest bit. And that's behind you. You get to fall off the change wagon and get back on as many times as you like. It's not only normal—it's inevitable.

Maintenance

Eventually, however, with enough persistence and hard work, along with the right tools, information and support, it is entirely possible to make it into the maintenance stage of change.

This is where it clicks. You finally realise, once and for all, how your new life is better than your old one. When you face a choice about whether to adopt the new, healthy habit or retain the old one, you know—in your bones—that the new way is better. Any short-term relief you might have once felt from the old habit (spending mindlessly) is replaced by the desire you feel to get the benefits of the new habit (joy and confidence in your money and financial skills).

That's where I now live when it comes to managing my money. And it's where I would like you to get to too, if you so choose.

●●●

Criticisms of the Stages of Change model I've just outlined include that it fails to take into account people's social context and socio-economic background. It fails to acknowledge that it's harder for some people to change than others, depending on their income level and social roles as mothers, fathers, carers or friends.

It's true that the company you keep heavily influences your behaviours. That's why it's so important, if you can, to find a friend to join you on this journey or, if you're in financial distress, to seek appropriate support from financial counsellors or others.

And no-one is saying you can think your way out of severe financial trouble. People on low incomes, or even living in poverty, may still get some benefit out of tracking their spending. But that won't pay the bills. There's only so much you can cut. Reaching out to local charities and not-for-profits for support can be vital.

However, for those making a decent living, and who are willing to try, I have seen the behaviour of tracking your spending yield great results. Many people tell me how eye-opening it is—whether it's the chocolate habit they didn't realise was so costly or the mother who didn't realise the kids were spending up quite so big on the parental credit card. It all adds up.

Changing your relationship with money

Before we move on, I want to mention some more concepts from psychology that may prove helpful as you set about developing new money habits.

First is the idea of identifying whether you have a 'growth' or a 'fixed' mindset when it comes to your life. We can thank a psychologist called Carol Dweck for this. Dweck has shown through numerous studies how adopting a growth mindset can positively impact performance, both of sportspeople and of others. Those who believe they are born with a set of inherent traits — 'I'm not good with money', for example — tend to act out those traits. Those who adopt a growth mindset believe they can change and improve their traits with enough practice.

I call it the 'yet' addendum, which is to say you can simply add the word 'yet' to anything you think you are stuck at — for example, 'I'm not good at money *yet*'.

Second, is embracing the idea of setting a 'change date'. Various psychological studies of addicts have found setting a firm date on which a new healthy habit will commence is beneficial. You see this commonly around the new year. There's something powerful about the new year, or even a new month, that human beings find compelling. Harness it. If you read this book towards the end of the month, commit to start tracking your spending on the first of whatever next month is.

The third and final psychological tool I'll mention here is the idea of 'self-monitoring'. Patients with mood disorders or depression are commonly asked to keep a mood diary to help identify trends or triggers. Food addicts are often asked to fill in a food journal. Why? Because knowing someone else is going to see your information can be a powerful motivator for making better decisions. Better yet is to be accountable and honest with yourself about your behaviours.

When it comes to money, I think tracking your own spending can act as a powerful self-monitoring tool.

If you can organise a monthly meet-up with friends who are also keen to track their spending, all the better. Yes, it's intimate, but the more we normalise money conversations, the better off we'll all be. And if you can't convince your friends, you've got me. Find me on Insta — @moneywithjess — and hang out with me as I review my monthly spending.

Choose to change your life

If you're anything like me, it's possible you've spent much of your life on autopilot, unaware of your power to choose the life you want.

Well, I'm here to tell you that you *can* change your relationship with money and you *can* improve your situation.

I guess that's the starting point of all self-help/personal-development books. But you really do have to believe it is possible first. And I hope you can get there.

I see so many people who seem to be stuck in the mindset of epiphenomenalism: thinking their money is just some external thing that they are witnessing but have no control over.

In my experience, life tends to eventually drag many of such people kicking and screaming to the point where they do have to change, be it due to overwhelming debt, a relationship breakdown, or a job loss or change.

The most powerful moments of change in life come when you realise you can choose to change your life — that you have actually been choosing this whole time and that you can choose differently.

Choosing differently can, however, be difficult. You may disappoint people who want you to act otherwise: friends who want to go out for dinner, for example. In fact, you may need to choose new friends, which is difficult in and of itself.

Choosing differently when it comes to money may also involve denying some of your own desires — usually the short-term ones — in return for long-term gain.

Your mission, should you choose to accept it, is to start weighing the costs and benefits of all your spending, not only for Today You, but also for Future You.

We can throw our hands up with the epiphenomenalist philosophers of this world. Or we can side with the psychologists. And, after some reflection, I know which side I'm on.

So where are you at? Still on the train or standing by the tracks?

Are you ready to make a change?

Let's do this.

CHAPTER 2:

CREATE A
MONEY MINDMAP

I may not have studied psychology, but I have certainly experienced events in my life that have led me to seek the support of professionals who have.

I used to feel a lot of shame about this, which, through the course of therapy, I've managed to pin down to a reoccurring thought that seeking mental health support meant I was broken in some way: defective, unlovable and unworthy.

I've since been able to reframe things and replace that thought with more helpful ones that make me feel (almost) proud that I do seek support. Namely, that seeking support just means I'm a flesh-and-blood human being. I'm a person who is worthy of support. I'm a person who cares enough for myself that I seek support when I need it.

A complex relationship can exist between money and mental health.

Chaos in your mind can manifest as chaos in your finances and vice versa: chaos in your finances can amplify chaos in your mind. It can be a chicken-or-egg problem and I definitely recommend seeking the support of a trained mental health support worker to help you with your unique situation.

But I also know therapy is a privilege many may not be able to afford.

Which is why I'm so happy to share in this chapter some of the simple lessons about emotions that I've learned over my years in therapy: where emotions arise from and how you can reframe your thinking to ease the intensity or frequency of challenging emotions, while also opening a door to experiencing more of the enjoyable emotions.

In this chapter, I'll run you through a series of exercises and worksheets designed to help you identify both the emotions you feel towards money and the underlying thoughts driving those emotions. We'll then seek to reframe any negative thoughts into more helpful statements that you can use as affirmations to put you in a more constructive mindset when it comes to managing your money.

Basically, we'll look at your current money mindmap and then we'll spring clean it a little to make sure it's helpful.

There are four steps to creating a money mindmap.

Step 1: Identify your money emotions

Readers of *Money with Jess* will remember my hilarious—or slightly sad, depending on what level of emotional insight you have—anecdote about the time my psychologist asked me to describe how a certain situation made me *feel*. I responded that it made me feel 'analytical'. Friends, that's not a feeling.

Turns out, not everyone has a natural and instinctive connection to what they are feeling in any given moment. Or rather, sometimes we lack the sufficiently nuanced vocabulary required to express our true feelings.

Which is why I love the following chart, which shows what a dazzlingly complex array of emotions we human beings are capable of feeling—and believe me, it's just the tip of the iceberg.

The emotions wheel

In *Money with Jess*, I asked readers to use the emotions wheel to help pinpoint their feelings about even just hearing the word 'money'.

And I'm about to ask you to do the same. But first, let me explain why starting with identifying your feelings is such a powerful thing.

Feelings are a powerful alarm system. They are the internal response we have to situations and things around us, and, more specifically, the thoughts we have about those situations and things.

It is possible to feel many emotions at once—for example, sadness at the passing of a loved one, but happiness for the life they lived.

Looking at the emotions wheel on the next page and pinpointing how you feel about money can be a powerful pointer not only to your true feelings, but also to what underlying thoughts might be causing those feelings.

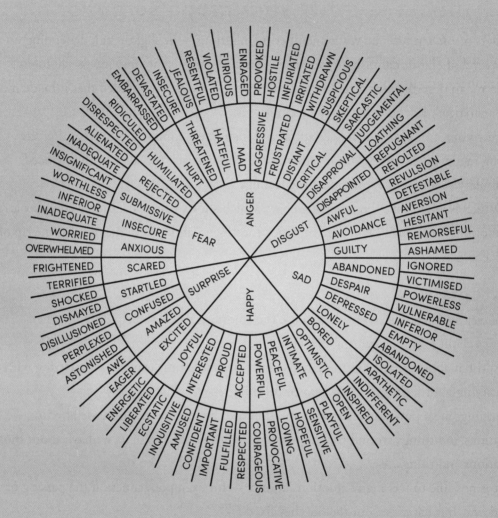

Spoiler alert: the emotions you feel about money—be they fear, overwhelm or shame—always derive from certain thoughts you're thinking about money, such as 'I'm bad at money', 'It's too late to make a difference' or 'I don't have enough money'.

Now, don't get me wrong: there may be an element of truth to some of those thoughts. But overall they are just not helpful … which we'll get to.

But first, look at the next page to see the very first (of many) worksheets you will find in this diary. Filling out these worksheets will be key to your progress. In fact, please don't continue reading this book until you have picked up a pen (you can do it!) and filled out the following worksheet. I don't want to sound pushy, but you simply *must* confront your feelings about money before we can make any progress. So do it now.

Go on. Skip to the next page and then come back here afterwards, ok …

Well done.

The thing about emotions, as we've discussed, is that they don't just spring out of nowhere. They are the body's response to our mental thoughts about the world around us.

Often, these thoughts are not conscious, but rather buried deep in our subconscious and can take some teasing out. But trust me, underneath every difficult emotion you have—and also the more pleasurable ones—you'll find, if you look hard enough, a thought.

Step 2 of creating your money mindmap is to identify your predominant money thoughts.

MY MONEY EMOTIONS

Look at the emotions wheel on page 14. Write down the feelings you experience when you think about money. Don't overthink this, and don't judge yourself for the emotions you currently gravitate to. It's okay to feel a mix of emotions from across the wheel. Just write down the feelings that jump out most to you. I'll wait …

MY CURRENT MONEY FEELINGS ARE

Now, look at the wheel and write down the emotions you want to feel about money.

MY DESIRED MONEY FEELINGS ARE

That wasn't so hard, was it? Well done you. Confronting your feelings can be an intimidating thing. But so important. I'm proud of you.

Step 2: Identify your money thoughts

Have a read through the following list of thoughts, which I find are quite commonly held about money. While you're at it, tick any you agree with. Again, don't overthink it. Go with your gut.

Money thoughts

- ☐ I'm bad at money.
- ☐ I've left it too late to get on top of my finances.
- ☐ I'll never have enough money.
- ☐ Money is just too complex for me to understand.
- ☐ Spending money is bad and I'm not supposed to do it.
- ☐ I should be saving more.
- ☐ There is a perfect way to do money and I'm failing.
- ☐ Managing money is just boring and I'd rather watch Netflix.

For each statement that resonates with you, try to identify an emotion that would be caused by holding that thought and jot it down next to the statement. It could be shame, fear, hopelessness, overwhelm, anxiety or guilt, just to name a few. Use the emotions wheel if you get stuck.

Now here's the mind twist.

Sometimes, our unhelpful thoughts about money actually stem from even deeper unhelpful thoughts we have (often without knowing it) about our capacities as a person. I have listed some common ones I see (and some I have felt myself) overleaf. Again, tick any that resonate for you (who doesn't love a good list to tick, right?).

Unhelpful thoughts

- ☐ I am broken.
- ☐ I am weird.
- ☐ There is something wrong with me.

- ☐ I am too much.
- ☐ I am not enough.
- ☐ I am unlovable.
- ☐ I am unworthy.

Ooft, right?

Again, holding any of these thoughts about yourself will lead to feelings of sadness, loneliness, isolation and unworthiness.

And we are not doing that anymore.

The good news is, once we can identify these thoughts, it is entirely possible to teach ourselves new ones — both about money and ourselves. So try these instead, you beautiful human you (again, with many borrowed directly from my own personal positive affirmations bank).

Helpful thoughts

- ☐ I am not broken. I am beautiful and whole. I am exactly as I am meant to be.
- ☐ I am not weird. I am excellent.
- ☐ I am loved by many people. They wish me well — to be at peace and succeed.
- ☐ I am a person who is mindful of my mental and emotional limits and I set firm boundaries with people to protect and nurture my inner peace.
- ☐ I am worthy of love, including the love I choose to show myself.
- ☐ I have inherent worth, just by existing.
- ☐ I am enough.

Seriously, lovely. You are.

Which brings us to the third step to creating your new and improved money mindmap.

Step 3: Reframe your negative money thoughts

Here is a list of helpful thoughts you could adopt when it comes to thinking about your money. Tick the ones you'd like to think in the future. We'll use them in the next exercise.

Helpful money thoughts

- ☐ Money is just a tool, and I am in control of how I use it.
- ☐ Money gives me the freedom to walk away from partners and workplaces that no longer serve me.
- ☐ I have developed a unique and valuable skillset and I will find a job/career in which it is correspondingly remunerated.
- ☐ I choose to release myself from guilt and regret when it comes to money.
- ☐ I can begin saving *today* if I simply spend less than I earn.
- ☐ I get to choose how I spend my money.
- ☐ I am growing stronger every day.
- ☐ Every new day is a chance to do better.
- ☐ I can choose how I decide to think about money.
- ☐ Money is not a measure of my worth.
- ☐ I am truly capable of having an excellent relationship with my money and I commit 100 per cent to the behaviours that will get me there — that is, regularly tracking my spending and checking my balances.

What emotions arise when you review this list? Hope, perhaps? Optimism, openness, confidence, empowerment?

In the next worksheet, we're going to take any negative money thoughts you are still harbouring and flip them into more helpful thoughts like those listed above.

MY NEW MONEY THOUGHTS

The idea, when reframing negative thoughts, is to simply witness them as they arise (which is often the hardest part) and then re-state them in the opposite. When you do this, you'll realise the opposite of a negative thought is, in fact, what many people would call an 'affirmation'.

Reciting affirmations daily out loud has been shown to have tangible and positive impacts on mood and mental health. I have a list that I used to read out daily. I now just dip into it as needed. If that's too woo-woo for you, just call them 'new money thoughts'. Whatever works for you. If you're really stumped, pick a few of the unhelpful thoughts you ticked on page 18 and simply rewrite them in the positive.

If you end up with some blank spaces, that's okay too. In the future, if you notice yourself having a negative thought about your money, you can come back and add to the list.

OLD THOUGHT	NEW THOUGHT
I am just a person who is bad at money.	With enough time and effort, I can teach myself a new way to be with money.
I'll never have enough money.	Little by little, I can work towards consistently spending less than I earn and slowly building my savings.

Step 4: Take 'opposite action'

Another reason why emotions are so powerful and so important to identify is that they each come with what psychologists call an 'action urge', or an urge to take some form of action, usually either avoidance or approach.

Fear makes us run away. Love makes us approach. Hopelessness makes us shut down. Inspiration draws us out.

When it comes to more challenging emotions, such as fear and anger, following our action urge may feel good in the short term. However, we know that simply following our automatic urges, like running away when you're scared, can simply heighten how often you will keep feeling that emotion in the long run.

We must stand and face our fears—if it is safe to do so, of course.

Deciding to act against our natural action urges is yet another tool in the therapeutic tool belt. Yes, I still think it's always a great idea to examine your thoughts and reframe them to reduce the occurrence of difficult emotions. But sometimes, that's just not enough.

You can also approach things from the other side by simply acting in opposition to your emotional urge.

Reframing your thoughts is a top-down approach, whereas just choosing to alter your behaviour is like a bottom-up approach. They both get you to the same outcome— changed behaviour—and you can decide what works best for you. Or do both!

In the 1970s, psychologist Marsha M Linehan pioneered the field of dialectical behaviour therapy (DBT), which has many aspects, one of which is to take 'opposite action'.

When we feel the emotion of shame, for example, the action urge is to hide or avoid sharing the underlying cause of our shame. Opposite action theory would say to tell your secret to people you can safely trust to accept it.

Sadness may drive us to withdraw or to isolate ourselves, but opposite action theory would urge us to get active and get out there—in tolerable amounts, of course.

Similarly, fear makes us want to run away or avoid something. So the opposite action would be to approach the fearful subject to some degree.

In the context of fears, this is also sometimes referred to as 'exposure therapy'. Say you're scared of spiders. First, you might try reframing your thoughts about spiders to something more helpful, such as 'spiders are wonderful creatures that protect me from flies'. In the likely event that that should prove insufficient to alleviate your fear, you might instead try 'opposite action' therapy by exposing yourself in small steps to spiders.

The first step might be to simply look at a cartoon picture of a spider and try to hold it in your hand. You might then progress to holding a picture of an actual spider. Then you might watch a video, all the way up to actually touching a … *No. Wait. Ew. Yuck. Stop right there.* We are not touching spiders.

But the example is relevant. My whole money management system is designed on the premise that many people probably like tracking their money as much as they like thinking about holding spiders. So to get you up and running, we make it fun, and colourful, and paper-and-pen based. Personally I actually love this process so much and I can't wait to show you how it works. But I know there are a few mental leaps to go before you get from fearing to loving your money. And I'm patient. I can wait.

So for those of you who have identified fearful feelings around money, the main message is this: you can't avoid your fear by avoiding your money. In fact, you are likely going to make things far worse by ignoring or failing to face up to your money situation.

Running away and never looking at or thinking about your bills, bank statements or credit card statements is a recipe for disaster. You may miss bills or fall behind—and you will likely still spend quite a bit of time feeling worried about money. The opposite action? Rip those letters open. Find those log-in details for your money accounts. Better yet, commit to actually using this money diary to track, in colourful baby steps, where your money is going.

The overall end goal here is to reduce the amount of time you spend stuck in difficult emotional states. You won't always be happy—some challenging states will still arise.

But you can witness them and either reframe them or take opposite action to overcome them.

In this way, you can reduce some of the suffering you feel about money, yes, and many other things in life too.

Now exhale.

CHAPTER 3:

TAKE YOUR MONEY 'BEFORE' SNAPSHOT

All right, I feel like we're getting on a bit of a roll here with the worksheets! Look at you go, confronting your fears and vowing to take opposite action. Amazing.

Now, I want you to stand naked in front of a mirror.

OMG, I'm kidding! (Although, if you are rocking your body positivity, go for it!) I actually just want you to stand metaphorically naked in front of a metaphorical mirror—only your body is your current money situation and the mirror is this diary. Phew!

But, don't exhale completely because you may still find this bit a little confronting. We are about to rip the band-aid off and actually have a look at where you are at with your money.

Anyone who has tried any weight-loss program knows that taking your 'before' snapshot is often a key recommended action. We're not into body shaming here, any more than we are into money shaming. But having some idea of your starting point when it comes to your money can certainly be helpful.

If you're trying to figure out where you want to go (which we'll do in the next chapter) you need to have some idea of your starting point.

So, we're going to do a quick stocktake of where you're at with your money—otherwise known as a 'net worth statement'.

Now, don't be intimidated. This is not as technical as it sounds, but rather a simple statement of everything you own versus everything you owe to other people, be it a bank or another lender.

You do not want the first time you do this exercise to occur in the middle of divorce proceedings. You also do not want to leave this task to your kids or partner to figure out in the event of your death. We are tidying up and getting a clearer picture of your total finances here. Not just for your own financial independence, but so that you can communicate this important information with loved ones.

If that's not motivation enough, I found $50 in an old bank account doing this! Like rooting around the back crevices of the couch ... you never know what you might find!

And if it all still seems overwhelming, remember that your net worth today (your assets minus your liabilities) is simply a lagging indicator of all the earning, spending and saving habits you've developed to date. And if you don't like what you see, you can change it.

Also remember this is *not* an exercise in determining your overall worth as a person—only your financial net worth. They're not the same. Keep that at the forefront of your mind.

To get you started, here's a non-exhaustive list of some of the types of assets you may own and might consider rummaging around to find evidence of:

- Principal residence
- Investment property
- Retirement accounts/super
- Shares
- Money in savings accounts
- Money in transaction accounts
- Money in cashback or rewards programs
- Actual cash in wallet or piggy bank
- Cars and vehicles
- Furniture and personal effects/belongings

- Unused gift cards
- Valuable items like sports or recreation items
- Artwork
- Currency
- A human body and mind capable of producing income—hey, it's priceless, but worth mentioning if you don't have much of the above!

Don't forget *you* are your most valuable asset. Look after yourself with regular sleep, good nutrition and movement. It may just be the best financial decision you ever make.

Now, when it comes to putting a figure on the value of your financial assets, value any items at their current market value—that is, what you would get from selling them today—not what you paid for them or what it would cost to replace them. Value your debts at the total outstanding amounts as of today.

You should be able to find most of the information you need in your bank accounts, savings accounts, loan documents, credit card statements and retirement accounts, although you might have to take a stab at the value of some assets, like property.

Now, here's a list of liabilities for you to consider:

- Credit cards
- Mortgages
- Investment loans
- Personal loans
- Vehicle loans
- Student loans
- Tax debts
- Buy-now-pay-later purchases
- Payment plans
- Overdue bills
- Unpaid fines or penalties
- Money owed to friends or family
- Payday loans
- Medical debts or payment plans
- Other.

Okay, it's time to fill in your money 'before' snapshot (see the next page).

This will give you an idea of where you're at with your money: what you own versus what you owe. At the end of the year, you can revisit these figures to see how far you've come (see part 3).

If the numbers aren't great, don't worry. The younger you are, the more you can expect to owe versus own. This is normal and to be expected.

For those approaching retirement, hopefully you are closer to building some wealth. And if not, remember it is never too late to take small steps and reach out for help and support if you need it. You're worth it, remember?

MY MONEY 'BEFORE' SNAPSHOT

Fill in as much information as possible about your current assets and debts. If you don't know exact values, just get your best estimate down on paper. In part 3, we'll revisit this and hopefully see some positive changes.

Date: ....

WHAT I OWN...

Asset	Estimated value
	$
	$
	$
	$
	$
	$
TOTAL	$

WHAT I OWE...

Liability	Amount
	$
	$
	$
	$
	$
	$
	$
TOTAL	$

MY NET WORTH

What I own minus what I owe: $ ....

CHAPTER 4

DREAM BIG, BABY!

Hello again, beautiful. It's me, Jess. Are you still with me? I am so proud of you for getting through the last chapter. I know how confronting looking at where you're at with your money can be. If you're not exactly enamoured with the financial image staring back at you in your money 'before' snapshot, that's more than fine.

Just remember you are about to join me on a marvellous adventure to track and take control of your cash flow—which will, if you keep at it, improve your ability to save and build wealth. But before we get there, I want you to take a moment to think big: what are you saving for, anyway?

I know you are reading this book because you are in some way dissatisfied with your financial life. We've done some great work to uncover your money mindmap and figure out your current situation. But rather than just running from that, you want to know what you're running towards.

If you really struggle to project forward to figure out on a blank sheet where you want your life to go, I see you. Sometimes, the art of creating your dream life involves having a crack at your current one and beginning to reflect on what you do and do not like about it. And that's what you'll be doing in chapter 8 (the diary itself) by examining your spending.

But I'd like to push you to try to go a little further forward now, if I may, because it's never too early, I believe, to start dreaming about the life you truly want to create with your precious time and money.

To do that, this chapter has three exercises that will help you dream big—*before* we get down to actually sorting you out with an achievable money goal in the next chapter.

The first exercise is to create a 'pleasures list' of things you currently enjoy (you'll find that on page 30).

In the early days of seeking therapy, one of my therapists asked me to draft a list of all the things I enjoyed doing. I was completely dumbfounded. I had no idea where to start. Often, we prioritise the needs of all the other people in our lives and we forget to focus on what brings us joy. We forget ourselves. Well, no more, beautiful.

Go ahead and create your very own 'pleasures list' on the next page — and try to make sure you do at least one thing from the list every day!

On the page after that one, you'll find the second of my 'dream big' exercises, which is to identify your highest life values. Just like identifying emotions, sometimes people lack the appropriate vocabulary they need to identify what they truly value in life, be it health or education or freedom.

When you spend your money, the first step should obviously be to make sure your purchases bring you some pleasure. But it's also important to try to ensure your spending is in alignment with your deeper sense of what is valuable in life.

Sure, going out and dropping $100 on dinner and drinks may be pleasurable in the short term. But if that conflicts with your longer-term values about attaining financial freedom or nurturing your health, you may want to think more deeply about your purchases.

To help you think bigger about your dream life, I've included a worksheet on page 31 where you can identify your life values. You can come back to this page to keep honing your values at any time.

After that, to finish off the chapter, we're going to complete my final 'dream big' exercise, which is to map your perfect day. Ultimately, how much money you need depends entirely on what lifestyle you desire to live today, and in the future. Keep things relatively simple, and you may not need to work as long or as hard as otherwise.

So, what does your dream day look like? Are you taking expensive holidays? Or finding pleasure in small daily routines like going for an evening walk or reading a book? Your vision for your dream day will not only help to inform your future savings goals, but it can also be used to search for clues to how you might start living better today.

Armed with your pleasures list, your life values and your perfect day, hopefully you will finish this chapter with a better sense of where you want to head with your financial future.

Take your time with each exercise. Repeat them as often as you like, but at least annually. As you use this diary, you will continue to improve your sense of what brings you joy and what vision you have for your future dream life.

You get to choose your life, remember? And you can choose differently any time you like.

So go on, dream big…

DREAM BIG, BABY!

MY PLEASURES LIST

Create a list of all the activities, things or people that bring you pleasure in life. If you can only name a few to start with, that's okay. As you use this diary over the year, come back to this page and add any purchases or experiences you encounter that bring you true joy.

You get bonus points for any pleasures you can identify that are free—that's a win win in my book.

To kick you off, here are a couple of examples from my own personal 'pleasures list':

♡ Coconut-scented hair conditioner

♡ Rewatching Lord of the Rings

♡ Salted pretzel chocolate

♡ Spending time with my loved ones

♡

♡

♡

♡

♡

♡

♡

♡

♡

♡

♡

♡

♡

♡

♡

♡

♡

♡

MY LIFE VALUES

On this page you'll find a comprehensive list of potential life values. Without overthinking it, circle all the ones you like. Then narrow it down to your top three. The better you can become at identifying your life values and aligning them to your actions—including how you spend your money—the happier you will be. Bonus points if you can find an intersection between your life values and your pleasures list. For example, I love reading books, and 'education' is one of my highest life values, so books get a green light in my budget. Ditto gym classes, which align with my value of 'health'. What do you value?

Achievement	Determination	Honesty	Prosperity
Adventure	Discipline	Humility	Responsibility
Affection	Diversity	Humour	Security
Ambition	Education	Imagination	Self-actualisation
Authenticity	Empathy	Independence	Self-development
Awareness	Endurance	Inner harmony	Self-reliance
Balance	Enthusiasm	Integrity	Self-respect
Beauty	Equality	Intelligence	Selflessness
Boldness	Excellence	Joy	Silence
Bravery	Exploration	Justice	Simplicity
Calmness	Fairness	Kindness	Spirituality
Caring	Family	Knowledge	Stewardship
Challenge	Fidelity	Learning	Strength
Charity	Fitness	Love	Structure
Comfort	Freedom	Loyalty	Surprise
Commitment	Fun	Mastery	Tolerance
Compassion	Generosity	Openness	Toughness
Connection	Grace	Optimism	Traditional
Contribution	Gratitude	Order	Tranquillity
Courage	Growth	Passion	Transparency
Creativity	Happiness	Patience	Understanding
Curiosity	Hard work	Playfulness	Wealth
Dependability	Health	Professionalism	Wisdom

MY TOP THREE LIFE VALUES

....

MY PERFECT DAY

Before we move on to setting firm goals in the next chapter, here is some space to help you map out your perfect day. If money were no object, how would you choose to spend your perfect day?

Who would you spend time with? What would you do? Would you work? What sport or movement would you participate in? Would you meditate? Journal? Run a business? Join a circus?

Personally I'd like to get up at dawn—around 6 am—have a coffee and do a workout. I'd eat breakfast at home at 9 am and get down to two or so hours of writing or creating financial education content. I'd have lunch at noon and then maybe have a siesta, do a little reading, yoga or go on a bush walk. I'd have dinner at 5 pm, preferably with loved ones, and then maybe watch a TV show before heading to bed at 8 pm and winding down, reading a little, snuggling a little and turning the lights off just after 9 pm.

Basically, I know what I'm doing in retirement. How about you?

6 am	
7 am	
8 am	
9 am	
10 am	
11 am	
12 pm	
1 pm	
2 pm	
3 pm	
4 pm	
5 pm	
6 pm	
7 pm	
8 pm	
9 pm	
10 pm	

CHAPTER 5

SET A MONEY GOAL

To be completely honest, I wasn't sure whether to include a chapter on goal setting. Most personal finance books start off by asking you to identify your money goal—whether it's paying off your credit card debts, saving up to buy your first home, learning how to invest or something else.

And these are very worthy goals indeed. But I also know they frequently just happen to induce a state of total overwhelm for a lot of people. The goals seem so impossibly large, it's hard to know which goal to choose or how to go about achieving it.

Sometimes, I think you're better off just committing to a process to observe your spending and then seeing what comes up. And if you'd prefer to do that, by all means skip ahead. This is the last chapter before the 'action' part of the book!

Still, for those brave enough to commit to a money goal, I do also believe they can act as a powerful motivator.

I've seen goal setting work both ways in my own life. On the positive side, I have, at various times in my life, successfully set new year's resolutions to write a book (tick), buy a home (tick) and run a marathon (tick).

But I've also frequently set weight-loss goals that were unattainable or fitness goals that simply didn't fit into my busy life at the time.

I've come to believe there are seasons in our lives when achieving big goals is fun and attainable, and others when we're simply swamped by the realities of earning an income, caring for family members and trying to enjoy life a little.

So, when planners begin by telling you to map your 'money goals' I'm extremely hesitant. Without some knowledge of your current financial set-up, spending habits and mindset, the risk of setting unachievable goals is very real.

I'm a big believer that your money habits—like tracking your spending and investing your surplus funds regularly—are more important than lofty or arbitrary goals.

If you choose the right habits, the goals have a way of looking after themselves. I believe you should focus on the habits and steps — like consistently spending less than you earn — that will get you to your bigger goals, rather than getting too fixated on the goals themselves.

However, I do know it's possible to have good habits and healthy goals, so ultimately I support setting goals as a worthy exercise.

To give yourself the maximum chance of success, I believe you must set goals that reflect your values, move you towards things you find pleasurable in life and are not too big at first.

If you want to achieve big things in life, it's almost certain you'll need to first achieve a series of small things.

When I first set my goal of buying a home — a prospect I admit I found overwhelming at first — I began by breaking my goal down into steps. Then, I selected the tiniest step possible, which was simply to walk into some banks on high street to ask about getting a loan. Buying a home is a big money goal. Walking into a bank and having a chat? That could be achieved in a day.

If you're struggling to know where to start with deciding what money goals are appropriate or achievable for you, getting some professional advice can really help. But in lieu of that, here's a list of what might be worthy financial goals for you to choose from.

My only ask is that you pick one — just one — to work on this year. If you're feeling super motivated, sure, pick multiple. Alternatively, simply decide on a goal to track your spending for one year using this diary: that would be enough to make me very happy.

If you feel comfortable to go bigger, consider this list.

A big money goals list

- [ ] Pay off high-interest debts such as credit cards, personal loans or car loans, either entirely or by a certain dollar amount.
- [ ] Start an emergency fund to cover unexpected expenses.
- [ ] Grow your emergency fund by a certain dollar amount.
- [ ] Save for a home deposit.
- [ ] Buy a home.
- [ ] Complete home renovations.
- [ ] Save for a holiday.
- [ ] Contribute extra to your retirement savings account.
- [ ] Learn how to invest in shares.
- [ ] Open a high-interest savings account.
- [ ] Use your surplus cash flow to apply for a property investment loan.
- [ ] Save up for a wedding.
- [ ] Save up for a baby/pet.
- [ ] Clear any buy-now-pay-later payments.
- [ ] Save money for Christmas.
- [ ] Save for a new car or to upgrade an old one using cash, not credit.
- [ ] Invest money in furthering your own education.
- [ ] Save for your kids' education.
- [ ] Invest on behalf of your kids.
- [ ] Start a business.
- [ ] Reduce your working hours or switch to part time.
- [ ] Make a donation to charity.

I'm fond of saying that goals are dreams with a deadline and a price tag attached. So, once you've selected your goal or goals (informed by your dreams), it's time to figure out an approximate total cost and a desired time frame for achieving each of your goals.

Then you can break down your goals into smaller milestones such as monthly amounts to save towards your goals.

On the following pages I've provided an example of a filled-out goal progress tracker for saving for a house deposit, and a blank worksheet for you to track the progress on one of your own goals—whatever that might be.

But just quickly, before you embark on this goal-setting exercise, I want to tell you about what's coming up next.

In part 1 we've considered where you're currently at with your money and created a vision of where you want to go. You've come so far and I'm incredibly proud of you!

The missing link is how to control your cash flow to achieve your goals—and that's what part 2 of this diary is all about. Other than inheriting great globs of money, the only reliable way to build your wealth is to spend less than you earn, consistently, over a long period and to invest any savings.

Once you do that, you can throw your surplus funds at whatever goal you choose—even if those goals evolve over time.

So spend some time using the next two pages and set up your own goal progress tracker, if you'd like to. You'll then be officially ready to make a change and to take action towards developing healthier money habits.

I can't wait to show you how to do it.

MY MONEY GOAL PROGRESS TRACKER

MY GOAL IS *Save $50,000 for a home deposit*

GOAL AMOUNT: **$50,000**
(debt to pay off, savings to build, amount to invest, etc.)

I'D LIKE TO ACHIEVE THIS BY: **In 4 years' time**

GOAL divided by 20 = **$2500** _____ (each bar represents this amount)

Shade in a bar for each increment you achieve!

$ 50 000
$ 47 500
$ 45 000
$ 42 500
$ 40 000
$ 37 500
$ 35 000
$ 32 500
$ 30 000
$ 27 500
$ 25 000
$ 22 500
$ 20 000
$ 17 500
$ 15 000
$ 12 500
$ 10 000
$ 7500
$ 5000
$ 2500

MY MONEY GOAL PROGRESS TRACKER

MY GOAL IS _____

GOAL AMOUNT: _____
(debt to pay off, savings to build, amount to invest, etc.)

I'D LIKE TO ACHIEVE THIS BY: _____

GOAL divided by 20 = _____ (each bar represents this amount)

Shade in a bar for each increment you achieve!

$
$
$
$
$
$
$
$
$
$
$
$
$
$
$
$
$
$
$
$

PART TWO

TAKE
ACTION

CHAPTER 6:

SET UP YOUR FUTURE FUNDS

One thing I have found very helpful in my personal budgeting journey is to try to smooth out any big, lumpy expenses that lob throughout the year. To do this, I sit down at the start of each year and set up what I call 'Future Funds'. The point of this is to set aside regular contributions towards large known or anticipated expenses, like my annual car service or annual home insurance.

If I don't do this, I find my monthly surpluses can swing wildly from month to month, or even swing into deficit.

So, at the start of the year I sit down with the worksheets at the end of this chapter and map out expected large expenses under a particular category, such as cars.

I list out all the expenses to come—such as rego, insurance, servicing, parts and repairs—tally them up and then figure out a monthly sum to direct towards savings. I then record this figure on my monthly budget summary sheet as monthly contributions under 'Expenses'. Generally, I do not change these monthly amounts throughout the year. If, at the end of the year, I realise I've overspent from a fund, I take the money from emergency savings (and replenish that from future monthly surpluses) or from any underused Future Funds that I may have.

Throughout the year, I track all 'drawdowns' from these funds on the individual Future Fund worksheets. I use the 'Future Fund drawdown' column on my spending tracker to note when I've used funds in this way, and as part of my end-of-month process, I make sure my individual fund tracking sheet is updated to note all these drawdowns.

And because I love highlighters I also draw a pretty picture on my fund worksheet to represent the category of expense (for example, I draw a car for my Car Future Fund) and colour in a bar for every month I've successfully made a contribution towards that fund (you'll see an example soon).

It gives me such peace of mind. I barely flinch anymore when I see huge bills hitting my accounts because I know I'm prepared.

Now here's the twist.

Currently, I don't actually set up separate bank accounts for each 'fund' or make regular transfers, or anything like that. All my money just sits in one bank account, which also houses my emergency savings, giving me a comfortable buffer should a large Future Fund drawdown come up before my contributions had time to accumulate sufficiently to cover it.

Basically, my Future Funds are just a powerful mental tool to 'hypothecate' some of the money sitting in my bank account for future use. So, if I see my balance creeping up, I don't spend it because I know that money is earmarked for a specific upcoming bill.

I think everyone should have at least two Future Funds: one for holidays and one for gift giving. When designing your gift-giving fund, don't forget Mother's Day, Father's Day, Christmas, birthdays, teacher presents and any other occasions you celebrate.

When planning your holiday future fund, consider all the trips you want to take over the year, and include all related expenses such as travel, accommodation, food, attractions, insurances and souvenirs. In the past, I've also used funds to save up for health expenses such as my annual skin check-up, household expenses such as quarterly body corporate fees on my apartment and education expenses such as school fees.

Go to the list of budget categories and subcategories on page 51 to see if there's anything you would like to start saving for via a Future Fund.

On the next page you'll find an example sheet of one of my previously completed funds to give you a steer.

If you really, really want to, you can just skip Future Funds altogether and get straight to tracking your spending.

Otherwise, at least give the four blank worksheets following my example a try for holiday and gift expenses. As part of your monthly budget summary, you can come back to these and track your contributions and drawdowns. And get creative with your drawings!

If you need more blank worksheets, you can download them from my website: jessicairvine.com.au/resources.

MY __TRANSPORT__ FUTURE FUND

Anticipated annual expenses

Expense	Estimated cost
rego	$ 400.00
insurance - CTP	$ 450.00
- comprehensive	$ 600.00
servicing + repairs	$ 500.00
parts + accessories	$ 500.00
roadside assist	$ 154.00
	$.
	$.
	$.
	$.
Total	$ 2604.00
Required monthly contributions:	$ 217.00

My monthly contributions progress tracker

J F M A M J J A S O N D

Drawdowns tracker

Date	Expense	Amount	Tally
15/11	service	$ 540.00	$ 540.00
19/11	CTP	$ 413.64	$ 953.64
21/11	rego	$ 388.00	$ 1341.64
29/11	roadside	$ 138.00	$ 1479.64
18/6	comp. ins.	$ 649.26	$ 2128.90
		$.	$.
		$.	$.
		$.	$.
		$.	$.
		$.	$.
		$.	$.
		$.	$.
		$.	$.
		$.	$.
		$.	$.
		$.	$.
		$.	$.
		$.	$.
		$.	$.
		$.	$.
		$.	$.
		$.	$.
		$.	$.
		$.	$.
		$.	$.

Annual drawdowns total: $ 2128.90

Balance at end of year (surplus/deficit): $ 475.10

MY .... FUTURE FUND

Anticipated annual expenses

Expense	Estimated cost
	$.
	$.
	$.
	$.
	$.
	$.
	$.
	$.
	$.
	$.
Total	$.
Required monthly contributions:	$.

My monthly contributions progress tracker

J	F	M	A	M	J	J	A	S	O	N	D

Drawdowns tracker

Date	Expense	Amount	Tally
		$.	$.
		$.	$.
		$.	$.
		$.	$.
		$.	$.
		$.	$.
		$.	$.
		$.	$.
		$.	$.
		$.	$.
		$.	$.
		$.	$.
		$.	$.
		$.	$.
		$.	$.
		$.	$.
		$.	$.
		$.	$.
		$.	$.
		$.	$.
		$.	$.
		$.	$.
		$.	$.
		$.	$.
		$.	$.
		$.	$.

Annual drawdowns total:	$.
Balance at end of year (surplus/deficit):	$.

MY .... FUTURE FUND

Anticipated annual expenses

Expense	Estimated cost
	$.
	$.
	$.
	$.
	$.
	$.
	$.
	$.
	$.
	$.
Total	$.
Required monthly contributions:	$.

My monthly contributions progress tracker

J	F	M	A	M	J	J	A	S	O	N	D

Drawdowns tracker

Date	Expense	Amount	Tally
		$.	$.
		$.	$.
		$.	$.
		$.	$.
		$.	$.
		$.	$.
		$.	$.
		$.	$.
		$.	$.
		$.	$.
		$.	$.
		$.	$.
		$.	$.
		$.	$.
		$.	$.
		$.	$.
		$.	$.
		$.	$.
		$.	$.
		$.	$.
		$.	$.
		$.	$.
		$.	$.
		$.	$.
		$.	$.
		$.	$.

Annual drawdowns total: $.

Balance at end of year (surplus/deficit): $.

MY .... FUTURE FUND

Anticipated annual expenses

Expense	Estimated cost
	$.
	$.
	$.
	$.
	$.
	$.
	$.
	$.
	$.
	$.
Total	$.
Required monthly contributions:	$.

My monthly contributions progress tracker

J	F	M	A	M	J	J	A	S	O	N	D

Drawdowns tracker

Date	Expense	Amount	Tally
		$.	$.
		$.	$.
		$.	$.
		$.	$.
		$.	$.
		$.	$.
		$.	$.
		$.	$.
		$.	$.
		$.	$.
		$.	$.
		$.	$.
		$.	$.
		$.	$.
		$.	$.
		$.	$.
		$.	$.
		$.	$.
		$.	$.
		$.	$.
		$.	$.
		$.	$.
		$.	$.
		$.	$.
		$.	$.
		$.	$.
		$.	$.

Annual drawdowns total: $.

Balance at end of year (surplus/deficit): $.

MY .... FUTURE FUND

Anticipated annual expenses

Expense	Estimated cost
	$.
	$.
	$.
	$.
	$.
	$.
	$.
	$.
	$.
	$.
Total	$.
Required monthly contributions:	$.

My monthly contributions progress tracker

J	F	M	A	M	J	J	A	S	O	N	D

Drawdowns tracker

Date	Expense	Amount	Tally
		$.	$.
		$.	$.
		$.	$.
		$.	$.
		$.	$.
		$.	$.
		$.	$.
		$.	$.
		$.	$.
		$.	$.
		$.	$.
		$.	$.
		$.	$.
		$.	$.
		$.	$.
		$.	$.
		$.	$.
		$.	$.
		$.	$.
		$.	$.
		$.	$.
		$.	$.
		$.	$.
		$.	$.
		$.	$.
		$.	$.
		$.	$.
		$.	$.

Annual drawdowns total: $.

Balance at end of year (surplus/deficit): $.

CHAPTER 7

HOW TO USE THIS DIARY

Congratulations! You are about to start taking control of your money in a serious way. Are you excited? A bit nervous? Don't worry, you'll be fine—I've got you. I will lead you every step of the way. ☺

In my previous book, *Money with Jess*, I outlined a method for compiling an annual budget that involved estimating all your annual expenses in advance. This is what I do each year, and if you're interested in giving that a try, do check out that book.

But there is another way.

An alternative method—the one you're about to embark on in this diary—is to simply start tracking your day-to-day spending and see how it all adds up.

For many people, I think the 'just start tracking' approach can be less intimidating than trying to confront everything in one go. Although it, too, can come with its own sense of trepidation—particularly if you've already identified that you have some fears around money.

By following the system I'm about to outline, you'll start identifying exactly where your money goes—perhaps for the first time.

While you may not like what you see, I can reassure you that you are not alone in this and that knowledge really is power. Seeing where your money is flowing *today* is the crucial first step to being able to direct it to go somewhere different *tomorrow*, should you wish.

I know that for some people, tracking their spending can feel a bit like rubbing a dog's nose in its mistakes. That's not the intention here—although, yes, it can be a real eye-opener about some of the places where you are perhaps over-indulging.

But rather than guilt-tripping yourself about your past spending, simply use it as information to direct you to better spending habits in the future.

If you ever get stuck or feel alone, jump onto my Instagram page (@moneywithjess) and you'll see me also plugging along, using this diary to track my spending and take control of my financial life.

You'll find your 12-month diary in chapter 8. Before you jump ahead to check it out (all right, one quick peek, but come straight back, okay?), in this chapter I'm going to explain the best way to fill in each month's worksheet. And then, in chapter 7, I'll teach you how to set up what I call 'Future Funds', which is my way of avoiding surprises whenever you encounter big expenses.

I'm so excited to have produced this diary so that I can use it alongside you. I think you're going to love it as much as I do.

Figuring out where your money's going

Yay, it's time to figure out where your dollars are going — from all the little daily purchases, like coffee or lunch at work, to the bigger things, like annual car insurance or quarterly water bills. We're going to capture them all as they occur.

In a nutshell, the process is to write down all your expenses as they occur and then, at the end of the month, we'll review, categorise and tidy them up into one neat little summary worksheet.

We'll also work slowly and methodically towards creating an annual snapshot on page 210 (you can also flick ahead and have a quick look if you like) to show you your money year in review.

But eyes on the road, friends. For now, we'll take it one step at a time.

The first thing to note is that you can start this diary in any month of the year. If you start midyear, say in June, simply complete the rest of the months to the end of the year and then flip back to the start of this diary to continue with January, February, and so on, of the next year. The important thing is to capture an entire year of living expenses. I know it can seem like a lot, but it's incredibly powerful information, I promise.

Here's is a quick list of the features you'll find in each month of the diary, which begins on page 61:

- My calendar (including monthly 'Jess' challenge' and habit tracker)
- Monthly intentions
- Monthly spending tracker

- Monthly budget summary
- Monthly reflections
- Monthly checklist.

Okay, now let's walk through the benefits of each feature in turn…

My calendar

There's nothing like being able to see your entire month ahead on one double-page spread.

Mark down any appointments you have, such as doctor or specialist appointments, along with birthdays and upcoming social events. Not only will this help you look forward to them, it will help you to plan for occasions that could end up being costly. If money is tight, you can then take action to shop around in advance for things you need to buy, like gifts, or, for social occasions, perhaps suggest cheaper alternatives like catching up for a walk rather than dinner.

If you like, you can also use this calendar to note down when any bills are due, or your incoming pay dates. I don't tend to do this myself, as I automate all my bill payments. But again, if money is tight, you may want to track your bill and pay cycles so you can feel more confident you have the money in the right place when you need it.

Crucially, the calendar pages are undated so you can use this diary in any year. Simply write in the numbers for the days in the circle at the top of each square. I've double — triple — checked that you'll always have enough space!

Jess' monthly challenge

On each calendar page, there's also a challenge from me to help you really focus on one particular category of spending at a time, be it food or holidays or cars. I provide you with a suggestion for an action you can take to either save some cash, or to improve your control over this area of your life. Give it a go and see if you can get the challenge done by the end of the month.

I'll be doing the challenges too, so tag me on Instagram (@moneywithjess) and share some of your wins!

Habit tracker

To keep you on track with any personal habits you are working on, such as moving your body each day, going to bed by 10 pm, drinking 2 litres of water, meditating or journaling (all the good stuff), I have included a 'Habit Tracker' on your calendar. Simply list any habits you want to track each month, and tick the corresponding circle each day once complete.

Monthly intentions

For the start of each month, I've designed a set of exercises to help you anticipate and look forward to the month ahead. Spend some time at the start of each month figuring out what you would like to get out of the month. You can also check in with your money emotions to see how you're tracking and how they're changing over time.

Monthly spending tracker

Now comes the really fun part! Starting on the first day of the month, write down every purchase you make—preferably as you make them or soon after so you don't get too behind. To spot patterns in your spending, you need to group your expenses into categories.

As I detailed in *Money with Jess*, I've gone to great trouble to scour statistical surveys of household spending to come up with the 10 budget categories I think really capture everything a human being could possibly spend money on. (We're not actually that different, when it comes down to it.)

On the following page, you'll find a complete list of my 10 categories and 80 subcategories of spending. (Not all of them will be relevant to you.) My book *Money with Jess* has an exhaustive breakdown of what to include under every category and subcategory (for example, toothpaste is in 'Household—hygiene' and paperclips are in 'Education—stationery'). So if you really want to get into the nitty gritty of my system, that's a good resource to refer to.

If you find yourself unsure of what to put where, use your intuition about what makes sense for you and stick to it throughout the year. The most important thing is that you do write down every expense and add it up over time. If you happen to put shampoo under 'Appearance—beauty products' and not 'Household—hygiene' (like I do) that's totally fine. You do you. Just try to do you consistently, okay?

THE 10 MONEY WITH JESS BUDGET CATEGORIES

Your job, should you choose to accept it, is to find 10 different-coloured highlighter pens and assign a colour to each of my 10 budget categories shown below.

Et voilà: you've just created your very own personalised colour code to use when highlighting your individual expenses by category on your spending tracker. Refer back to this page as needed to identify a category for each expense.

1 HOUSING

2 HOUSEHOLD

- Furniture
- Décor
- Appliances
- Home maintenance and repairs
- Cleaning
- Hygiene
- Garden
- Strata fees
- Home insurance
- Council rates
- Household services

3 UTILITIES

- Electricity
- Gas
- Water and sewerage
- Internet
- Phone
- Postal services

4 TRANSPORT

- Vehicle purchase
- Vehicle loan payments
- Vehicle registration
- Drivers licence
- Vehicle insurance
- Vehicle servicing and repairs
- Vehicle parts and accessories
- Roadside assist
- Driving lessons
- Fuel
- Tolls
- Parking
- Public transport
- Vehicle hire, taxis and ride shares

5 FOOD

6 HEALTH

- Health insurance
- Pet insurance and veterinary costs
- Doctors and specialists
- Dental
- Optical
- Hospital and ambulance
- Medicines
- Medical equipment
- Sport and fitness

7 EDUCATION

- Books, newspapers and magazines
- Stationery
- Home computer equipment
- Childcare
- School
- Higher education

8 APPEARANCE

- Clothes and shoes
- Accessories
- Hairdressing
- Beauty products
- Beauty treatments

9 LIFESTYLE

- Eating out and takeaway
- Alcohol
- Tobacco and drugs
- Holidays
- Seasonal celebrations
- Parties and functions
- Gifts
- Toys
- Streaming services
- Gaming and consoles
- Music, audio and photographic
- Live entertainment
- Attractions
- Hobbies
- Gambling
- Pet purchases

10 PROFESSIONAL FEES

- Credit cards
- Other loans
- Bank fees
- Life / trauma / TPD insurance
- Income protection insurance
- Financial advisor fees
- Accountant / tax agent fees
- Legal fees
- Funeral expenses
- Union / professional association fees
- Child support
- Pocket money
- Charity donations

How to fill in the spending tracker

Start by recording the date of your purchase in the first column on of the spending tracker.

Next, note the payment method you used in the second column. If it was 'cash', write cash. If it was an account or credit card, make a note of that. This is a good prompt to remember to check through all your accounts and payment methods to capture every expense.

In the third column, write a brief description of your expense (for example, 'train ticket', 'takeaway coffee', 'water bill').

In the fourth column, assign your expense to one of the 10 budget categories. In my example above, the categories would be 'Transport', 'Lifestyle' and 'Utilities'.

It can also be useful to note in your expense description which 'subcategory' your expense falls into.

For instance, I might write in my own tracker, 'train ticket — public transport', or 'coffee — eating out and takeaway' to help me easily sort and tally expenses for all subcategories at the end of the month on my monthly budget summary (more on this shortly). The annual spending review on page 210 also splits category expenses into subcategories, so it pays to familiarise yourself with these from the outset.

In the fifth column, write in the total spent.

'Jess, what about when I make a purchase of items spanning multiple subcategories in one transaction?' I hear you ask … Clever question, thank you. I can see you are really paying attention!

When you make a transaction, such as at the grocery store, that spans multiple subcategories — for example, 'food', 'cleaning supplies' and 'hygiene' — split the receipt out into how much was spent on each particular subcategory and record them as three (or whatever number) separate expenses on your tracker.

When doing this, I also use my highlighters to highlight the different category expenses on the printed receipt. Which is just. So. So. Fun. (I really should get out more. ☺)

MY SPENDING TRACKER

Here's an example of a page from my spending tracker fully filled in so you can see roughly how it works. And on the next page I'll explain what to put in each column of the spending tracker.

Date	Payment method	Expense	Category	Amount	Direct debit	Future Fund drawdown	Variable spending	Essential? Y/N	Entered?
1	"	pocket money	PROFESSIONAL FEE	$ 53 50			×	N	○
1	"	cloud storage	UTILITIES	$ 14 99	×			Y	○
1	"	wine	LIFESTYLE	$ 14 00			×	N	○
1	"	choc top	LIFESTYLE	$			×	N	○
1	"	dinner out	LIFESTYLE	$ 30 00			×	N	○
2	"	hair cut (Jess)	APPEARANCE	$ 2 21			×	N?	○
2	"	kids clothes	APPEARANCE	$ 36 95			×	Y	○
2	"	dinner out	LIFESTYLE	$ 9 10			×	N	○
2	"	bin bags . cleaning	HOUSEHOLD	$ 4 25			×	Y	○
2	"	panadol . medicine	HEALTH	$ 4 50			×	Y	○
2	"	food @ Coles	FOOD	$ 290 36			×	Y	○
4	"	health insurance	HEALTH	$ 81 29	×			Y	○
5	"	bus trip	TRANSPORT	$ 3 93			×	Y	○
7	"	public transport	TRANSPORT	$ 20 00			×	Y	○
9	"	take away	LIFESTYLE	$ 59 10			×	N	○
10	"	cruise downpaym.	LIFESTYLE	$ 1350 11		×		N	○
13	"	maccas	LIFESTYLE	$ 22 30			×	N	○
13	"	after school care	EDUCATION	$ 48 95			×	Y	○
14	"	internet	UTILITIES	$ 59 95	×			Y	○
15	"	mascara	APPEARANCE	$ 27 00			×	N	○
15	"	gift for friend	LIFESTYLE	$ 77 99	×			N	○
15	"	furniture	HOUSEHOLD	$ 69 00			×	N	○
15	"	decor (candles)	HOUSEHOLD	16 75			×	N	○
15	"	book	EDUCATION	12 00			×	N	○
16	"	school fees Term 3	EDUCATION	3338 50	×			N/N	○
16	"	food @ Coles	FOOD	206 16			×	Y	○
16	"	food @ Aldi	FOOD	$ 25 54			×	Y	○
16	"	alcohol @ Aldi	LIFESTYLE	$ 17 99			×	N	○

If you are unsure of your category or subcategory, refer back to the guide on page 51. I like to slip a $5 note into that page to use as a bookmark so I can find it!

In the next three skinny columns towards the end of the spending tracker, put a cross to denote whether the expense was a 'direct debit' (a payment made via permission you've given to a certain company to regularly deduct sums from your accounts), a drawdown from a 'Future Fund' (these are optional and outlined in the next chapter) or a 'variable expense' (which is everything else).

I like to separate out my expenses this way so I can easily keep track of my direct debtors (and shop around regularly to make sure I'm on the best deal for each of these) and also use my Future Funds to plan for big expenses.

If that all sounds like too much at this stage, you can just record everything as a variable expense or ignore these columns if you choose. Up to you.

The last column is a place to reflect on whether each purchase was essential or not. Mark each expense with a 'Y' for 'yes' or an 'N' for 'no'.

Don't overthink it; just go with your gut. I mark every eating out expense as 'N' because I could cook at home. Doesn't mean I shouldn't have spent the money, but it's a good little reminder to keep things in check.

Finally, there's a circle at the end of each line. Tick these off at the end of the month to confirm that you have tallied, or 'entered', each expense into your monthly budget summary (trust me: it's soooooo satisfying to tick off each expense as you tally it).

Monthly budget summary

Now add it all up!

I love my end-of-month process for figuring out how much money came in that month, how much went out and what surplus or deficit I was left with.

Why? Because then I get to decide what to do with any surplus amount, be it investing, paying off debt faster or putting it towards a long-term savings goal. Now you have space to do the same!

MY JANUARY BUDGET SUMMARY

INCOME

	$.		$.
	$.		$.

EXPENSES

Direct debits	Amount	Variable spending		Amount	
home loan min. repay.	$ 4022.00	HOUSEHOLD	·decor	$ 43	75
electricity	$ 103.71		·cleaning	$ 14	24
internet	$ 59.95		·hygiene	$ 10	96
cloud storage	$ 29.98		·furniture	$ 69	00
phone	$ 15.20		·appliances	$ 14	00
health insurance	$ 81.29	TRANSPORT	·petrol	$ 106	.17
gym	385 99		·public transport	103	93
	$.		·parking	$ 5	06
	$.		·tolls	$ 25	00
	$.	FOOD		$ 754	.13
Total direct debits	$ 4698.12	HEALTH	·medicine	$ 4	50
			·sport + fitness	$ 70	00

Future Fund contributions	Amount	EDUCATION	·books etc	$ 35	65
HOUSEHOLD	$ 620.00		·after school care	$ 135	34
TRANSPORT	$ 250.00	APPEARANCE	·hair (Jess)	$ 42	21
EDUCATION	$ 1200.00		·clothes (kid)	$ 36	95
GIFTS	$ 200.00		·beauty products	$ 27	00
HOLIDAYS	$ 1265.00		·clothes (Jess)	$ 8	40
HEALTH	$ 110.00	LIFESTYLE	·alcohol	$ 31	99
	$.		·eating out	$ 249	52
	$.	PROFESSIONAL FEES	·donation	$ 7	00
	$.		·pocket money	$ 53	50
Total Future Fund contributions	$ 3845.00	Total variable spending		$ 1848	30

TOTAL INCOME	$.	What I will do with this surplus	Amount
		Top up Emergency Fund	$.
TOTAL EXPENSES	$ 10 391.42	Buy shares	$.
			$.
AMOUNT LEFT	$.		$.

Yes, there's a bit of work involved in tallying your monthly expenses. But you'll get quicker over time, and the effort is well worth it, I promise.

Once assembled, you'll be able to use this information to powerful effect to apply for property or investment loans with confidence, figure out how much you need to save for retirement or plan an emergency fund of 'X' months of living expenses. One month is not enough to give you an accurate picture of your average monthly spending. But complete this process for a number of months, and a more accurate picture will emerge.

How to fill in the monthly budget summary

To fill in your monthly budget summary, start by scanning the 'direct debits' column of your spending tracker and listing down all your direct debits. Tick off each expense on your spending tracker once you have entered it on your monthly budget summary sheet.

Next, if you're using them, note down how much you're contributing to your Future Funds. I show you the process for figuring this out in the previous chapter. (If you're not using Future Funds, just ignore this step.)

Then, scan the variable expenses column in your spending tracker by colour and group them into their categories and subcategories. Start with Housing, then Household, then Utilities, and so on.

Tally the variable expenses by subcategory and enter each on a separate line in the column 'Variable spending' in your monthly budget summary. Highlight each entry with the relevant colour. While it's true there are a lot of subcategories, you'll soon realise you are only really using a few regular ones for variable expenses each month.

Next, add up all your direct debits, Future Fund contributions (if any) and variable spending to get your total spending for the month.

Moving on to the income side of your budget, write down all the income you received from all sources during that month, including salary, side hustles, share dividends, rent and government benefits.

Record the after-tax amount — that is, the amount you'll get to keep. If tax hasn't already been deducted from your payments, make sure you calculate an estimate of what that will be and put that amount aside in an account to cover any tax bill come tax time.

Then, deduct your expenses from your income to see if you are in surplus or deficit for the month!

Hopefully you'll have a surplus.

If you're in deficit, look for areas where you can potentially cut back next month. If you're in surplus, decide what you want to do with your surplus funds — you could pay off extra debt, increase your emergency fund / cash savings, invest outside of retirement accounts or invest in your retirement account or any extra options you choose. Oh, okay … if you've done really well in a particular month, go and spend a small amount on something you'd really like to spoil yourself with.

Monthly reflections

This is your space to reflect on the month gone by. Here you can record the nice things that happened which you may have forgotten already and also any achievements at work (this will help arm you with evidence for that next pay rise!).

Crucially, spend some time reflecting on which purchases in that month brought you particular joy and which ones, with the benefit of hindsight, you didn't really need or enjoy. This is all part of the process of honing your sense of joy, so you can make better purchasing decisions in the future.

There's also a bit of space on your reflections page for a money mindmap check-in, where you can have a think about your money thoughts — if you know what I mean — and identify any unhelpful thoughts you might need to reframe.

Monthly checklist

Finally, because you've done so well and come so far, I've rewarded you with an end-of-month checklist to remind you of all the work you've successfully completed. Who doesn't love a checklist, right?

And that's it, you're done for the month! On to the next month. ☺

Tips for staying on track

☐ Keep your diary somewhere within sight. Try to check it every day or every couple of days.

☐ Have a dedicated space where you fill in your diary, be it a desk or a favourite chair. Light a candle; make it a nice ritual!

☐ Buy an old-fashioned calculator. Yes, I know we have them on our phones, but there's nothing like the satisfaction of tapping the buttons on an old-school calculator as you complete your monthly budget summary — and it will help to stop you getting distracted by your phone.

☐ *Buy. The. Highlighters.* Buy 10 colours. Label them with their category name.

☐ Make it social. Why not host a monthly budget checking meetup with your friends to go over your numbers and compare? Accountability partners can be a powerful tool in creating new habits.

☐ Remember, you are observing, not judging yourself. Just write everything down. These are the facts of your life. And if you want to improve your life, you need to know them.

CHAPTER 8

YOUR MONEY DIARY

Okay, friends. It's time to start your money diary!

I'm so proud of all the hard work you've put in so far by examining your thoughts and emotions about money, and confronting your current money situation and where you want to go.

Now it's time for the rubber to really hit the road as you start to track your spending! But don't rush. We have time. A whole year, in fact.

All you need to do now is commit to filling in this diary and setting your intentions for the month, then tracking and categorising your spending, tallying it up and reflecting at the end of the month.

Just take it one page at a time.

If you get stuck or lose motivation at any point (it's likely you will, as we learned from the Stages of Change model), remember what this is all about: observing yourself and how you choose to allocate your money.

If you drop off with the tracking at any point because, you know, life happens, go back to your bank statements and pick up the trail again. If you get stuck remembering how to do anything, refer to chapter 6, which has all the instructions for using the diary. If you find a way to make the process work better for you, by all means go for it. And if you'd like some company, come and see me using the diary @moneywithjess.

I wish you all the best as you embark on this exciting journey of discovery about your money and yourself. All great journeys start with a single step. And you're about to take yours ...

Let's do this!

JANUARY

Beyond fear lies freedom

Jess' JANUARY CHALLENGE

The New Year is the perfect time to declutter your home! Transform your unwanted items into cash by selling something on Facebook Marketplace or Gumtree.

☐ **Challenge accepted**

HABIT TRACKER

○ **Habit 1**

○ **Habit 2**

○ **Habit 3**

○ **Habit 4**

○ **Habit 5**

MONDAY	TUESDAY	WEDNESDAY

THURSDAY	FRIDAY	SATURDAY	SUNDAY

MY JANUARY INTENTIONS

The three things I am most looking forward to this month:

_____

_____

_____

The top three events that could prove expensive:

_____

_____

_____

My top three priorities at work, study or in family life:

_____

_____

_____

Three fun things I could do this month that are free:

_____

_____

_____

The top three people I want to connect with this month:

_____

_____

_____

This month will be a success if I can look back and know that:

_____

_____

_____

How I am currently feeling about my money:

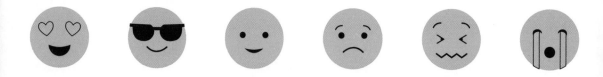

MY JANUARY SPENDING TRACKER

Date	Payment method	Expense	Category	Amount	Direct debit	Future Fund drawdown	Variable spending	Essential? Y/N	Entered?
				$.					○
				$.					○
				$.					○
				$.					○
				$.					○
				$.					○
				$.					○
				$.					○
				$.					○
				$.					○
				$.					○
				$.					○
				$.					○
				$.					○
				$.					○
				$.					○
				$.					○
				$.					○
				$.					○
				$.					○
				$.					○
				$.					○
				$.					○
				$.					○
				$.					○
				$.					○
				$.					○
				$.					○
				$.					○

Date	Payment method	Expense	Category	Amount	Direct debit	Future Fund drawdown	Variable spending	Essential? Y/N	Entered?
				$.					◯
				$.					◯
				$.					◯
				$.					◯
				$.					◯
				$.					◯
				$.					◯
				$.					◯
				$.					◯
				$.					◯
				$.					◯
				$.					◯
				$.					◯
				$.					◯
				$.					◯
				$.					◯
				$.					◯
				$.					◯
				$.					◯
				$.					◯
				$.					◯
				$.					◯
				$.					◯
				$.					◯
				$.					◯
				$.					◯
				$.					◯
				$.					◯
				$.					◯
				$.					◯
				$.					◯
				$.					◯
				$.					◯

Date	Payment method	Expense	Category	Amount	Direct debit	Future Fund drawdown	Variable spending	Essential? Y/N	Entered?
				$.					○
				$.					○
				$.					○
				$.					○
				$.					○
				$.					○
				$.					○
				$.					○
				$.					○
				$.					○
				$.					○
				$.					○
				$.					○
				$.					○
				$.					○
				$.					○
				$.					○
				$.					○
				$.					○
				$.					○
				$.					○
				$.					○
				$.					○
				$.					○
				$.					○
				$.					○
				$.					○
				$.					○
				$.					○
				$.					○
				$.					○
				$.					○

Date	Payment method	Expense	Category	Amount	Direct debit	Future Fund drawdown	Variable spending	Essential? Y/N	Entered?
				$.					○
				$.					○
				$.					○
				$.					○
				$.					○
				$.					○
				$.					○
				$.					○
				$.					○
				$.					○
				$.					○
				$.					○
				$.					○
				$.					○
				$.					○
				$.					○
				$.					○
				$.					○
				$.					○
				$.					○
				$.					○
				$.					○
				$.					○
				$.					○
				$.					○
				$.					○
				$.					○
				$.					○
				$.					○
				$.					○
				$.					○
				$.					○

Date	Payment method	Expense	Category	Amount	Direct debit	Future Fund drawdown	Variable spending	Essential? Y/N	Entered?
				$.					○
				$.					○
				$.					○
				$.					○
				$.					○
				$.					○
				$.					○
				$.					○
				$.					○
				$.					○
				$.					○
				$.					○
				$.					○
				$.					○
				$.					○
				$.					○
				$.					○
				$.					○
				$.					○
				$.					○
				$.					○
				$.					○
				$.					○
				$.					○
				$.					○
				$.					○
				$.					○
				$.					○
				$.					○
				$.					○

MY JANUARY BUDGET SUMMARY

INCOME			
	$.		$.
	$.		$.

EXPENSES

Direct debits	Amount	Variable spending	Amount
	$.		$.
	$.		$.
	$.		$.
	$.		$.
	$.		$.
	$.		$.
	$.		$.
	$.		$.
	$.		$.
Total direct debits	$.		$.
			$.
Future Fund contributions	**Amount**		$.
	$.		$.
	$.		$.
	$.		$.
	$.		$.
	$.		$.
	$.		$.
	$.		$.
	$.		$.
	$.		$.
Total Future Fund contributions	$.	**Total variable spending**	$.

TOTAL INCOME	$.	What I will do with this surplus	Amount
			$.
TOTAL EXPENSES	$.		$.
			$.
AMOUNT LEFT	$.		$.

MY JANUARY REFLECTIONS

The three best things that happened to me this month:

The three purchases that brought me the most joy:

My top three achievements at work or study:

The three things I bought that, in hindsight, didn't bring much pleasure:

MONEY MINDMAP CHECK-IN

A negative thought about money I noticed this month was:

This thought made me feel: _____ (refer to the emotions wheel)

Instead, I choose to flip this thought around and to think that:

How I am currently feeling about my money:

MY JANUARY CHECKLIST

I am proud to say that this month I successfully (tick as appropriate):

☐ Recorded every dollar I spent on my spending tracker

☐ Created a monthly summary of my income and expenses

☐ Calculated my monthly surplus or deficit

☐ If in surplus, I decided how to allocate my surplus funds between paying off debt, increasing my cash buffer or investing and I have completed any transfers of funds or purchases required to implement those decisions

☐ If using them, I updated my Future Fund worksheets (pages 43 to 46) to reflect my monthly contributions and spending drawdowns

☐ Filled out my monthly spending totals on my annual tally sheet on page 210 of this diary

☐ Completed this month's Jess' challenge

☐ Reminded myself that I am not perfect, but am committed to making small changes to improve my finances

FEBRUARY

*Start with small, actionable steps ...
then keep going!*

Jess' FEBRUARY CHALLENGE

	MONDAY	TUESDAY	WEDNESDAY

Did you know February is National Library Lovers' month? Pay a visit to your local library to access free books and inquire about which smartphone app you can use to access their digital collections at home.

☐ **Challenge accepted**

HABIT TRACKER

○ **Habit 1**

○ **Habit 2**

○ **Habit 3**

○ **Habit 4**

○ **Habit 5**

THURSDAY		FRIDAY		SATURDAY		SUNDAY	
	○		○		○		○
	○		○		○		○
	○		○		○		○
	○		○		○		○
	○		○		○		○
	○		○		○		○
	○		○		○		○
	○		○		○		○
	○		○		○		○
	○		○		○		○
	○		○		○		○
	○		○		○		○
	○		○		○		○
	○		○		○		○
	○		○		○		○
	○		○		○		○
	○		○		○		○
	○		○		○		○
	○		○		○		○
	○		○		○		○
	○		○		○		○
	○		○		○		○
	○		○		○		○
	○		○		○		○
	○		○		○		○

MY FEBRUARY INTENTIONS

The three things I am most looking forward to this month:

....

....

....

The top three events that could prove expensive:

....

....

....

My top three priorities at work, study or in family life:

....

....

....

Three fun things I could do this month that are free:

....

....

....

The top three people I want to connect with this month:

....

....

....

This month will be a success if I can look back and know that:

....

....

....

How I am currently feeling about my money:

MY FEBRUARY SPENDING TRACKER

Date	Payment method	Expense	Category	Amount	Direct debit	Future Fund drawdown	Variable spending	Essential? Y/N	Entered?
				$.					○
				$.					○
				$.					○
				$.					○
				$.					○
				$.					○
				$.					○
				$.					○
				$.					○
				$.					○
				$.					○
				$.					○
				$.					○
				$.					○
				$.					○
				$.					○
				$.					○
				$.					○
				$.					○
				$.					○
				$.					○
				$.					○
				$.					○
				$.					○
				$.					○
				$.					○
				$.					○
				$.					○
				$.					○

Date	Payment method	Expense	Category	Amount	Direct debit	Future Fund drawdown	Variable spending	Essential? Y/N	Entered?
				$.					◯
				$.					◯
				$.					◯
				$.					◯
				$.					◯
				$.					◯
				$.					◯
				$.					◯
				$.					◯
				$.					◯
				$.					◯
				$.					◯
				$.					◯
				$.					◯
				$.					◯
				$.					◯
				$.					◯
				$.					◯
				$.					◯
				$.					◯
				$.					◯
				$.					◯
				$.					◯
				$.					◯
				$.					◯
				$.					◯
				$.					◯
				$.					◯
				$.					◯
				$.					◯
				$.					◯
				$.					◯
				$.					◯

Date	Payment method	Expense	Category	Amount	Direct debit	Future Fund drawdown	Variable spending	Essential? Y/N	Entered?
				$.					○
				$.					○
				$.					○
				$.					○
				$.					○
				$.					○
				$.					○
				$.					○
				$.					○
				$.					○
				$.					○
				$.					○
				$.					○
				$.					○
				$.					○
				$.					○
				$.					○
				$.					○
				$.					○
				$.					○
				$.					○
				$.					○
				$.					○
				$.					○
				$.					○
				$.					○
				$.					○
				$.					○
				$.					○
				$.					○
				$.					○
				$.					○
				$.					○

Date	Payment method	Expense	Category	Amount	Direct debit	Future Fund drawdown	Variable spending	Essential? Y/N	Entered?
				$.					○
				$.					○
				$.					○
				$.					○
				$.					○
				$.					○
				$.					○
				$.					○
				$.					○
				$.					○
				$.					○
				$.					○
				$.					○
				$.					○
				$.					○
				$.					○
				$.					○
				$.					○
				$.					○
				$.					○
				$.					○
				$.					○
				$.					○
				$.					○
				$.					○
				$.					○
				$.					○
				$.					○
				$.					○
				$.					○
				$.					○

Date	Payment method	Expense	Category	Amount	Direct debit	Future Fund drawdown	Variable spending	Essential? Y/N	Entered?
				$.					○
				$.					○
				$.					○
				$.					○
				$.					○
				$.					○
				$.					○
				$.					○
				$.					○
				$.					○
				$.					○
				$.					○
				$.					○
				$.					○
				$.					○
				$.					○
				$.					○
				$.					○
				$.					○
				$.					○
				$.					○
				$.					○
				$.					○
				$.					○
				$.					○
				$.					○
				$.					○
				$.					○
				$.					○
				$.					○
				$.					○
				$.					○

MY FEBRUARY BUDGET SUMMARY

INCOME			
	$.		$.
	$.		$.

EXPENSES

Direct debits	Amount	Variable spending	Amount
	$.		$.
	$.		$.
	$.		$.
	$.		$.
	$.		$.
	$.		$.
	$.		$.
	$.		$.
	$.		$.
	$.		$.
Total direct debits	$.		$.
			$.

Future Fund contributions	Amount		Amount
	$.		$.
	$.		$.
	$.		$.
	$.		$.
	$.		$.
	$.		$.
	$.		$.
	$.		$.
	$.		$.
Total Future Fund contributions	$.	**Total variable spending**	$.

		What I will do with this surplus	Amount
TOTAL INCOME	$.		$.
			$.
TOTAL EXPENSES	$.		$.
			$.
AMOUNT LEFT	$.		$.

MY FEBRUARY REFLECTIONS

The three best things that happened to me this month:

....

....

....

The three purchases that brought me the most joy:

....

....

....

My top three achievements at work or study:

....

....

....

The three things I bought that, in hindsight, didn't bring much pleasure:

....

....

....

MONEY MINDMAP CHECK-IN

A negative thought about money I noticed this month was:

....

This thought made me feel: .... (refer to the emotions wheel)

Instead, I choose to flip this thought around and to think that:

....

How I am currently feeling about my money:

MY FEBRUARY CHECKLIST

I am proud to say that this month I successfully (tick as appropriate):

- ☐ Recorded every dollar I spent in my spending tracker

- ☐ Created a monthly summary of my income and expenses

- ☐ Calculated my monthly surplus or deficit

- ☐ If in surplus, I decided how to allocate my surplus funds between paying off debt, increasing my cash buffer or investing and I have completed any transfers of funds or purchases required to implement those decisions

- ☐ If using them, I updated my Future Fund worksheets to reflect my monthly contributions and spending drawdowns

- ☐ Filled out my monthly spending totals on my annual tally sheet on page 210 of this diary

- ☐ Completed this month's Jess' challenge

- ☐ Reminded myself that I am not perfect, but am committed to making small changes to improve my finances

MARCH

The best things in life are free

		MONDAY		TUESDAY		WEDNESDAY

Jess' **MARCH CHALLENGE**

Your social life doesn't have to break the bank! Create a 'fun and free' list of activities you enjoy doing, like going for a walk or visiting a museum, which do not cost a cent.

☐ **Challenge accepted**

HABIT TRACKER

○ **Habit 1**

○ **Habit 2**

○ **Habit 3**

○ **Habit 4**

○ **Habit 5**

THURSDAY		FRIDAY		SATURDAY		SUNDAY	
○ ○ ○ ○ ○		○ ○ ○ ○ ○		○ ○ ○ ○ ○		○ ○ ○ ○ ○	
○ ○ ○ ○ ○		○ ○ ○ ○ ○		○ ○ ○ ○ ○		○ ○ ○ ○ ○	
○ ○ ○ ○ ○		○ ○ ○ ○ ○		○ ○ ○ ○ ○		○ ○ ○ ○ ○	
○ ○ ○ ○ ○		○ ○ ○ ○ ○		○ ○ ○ ○ ○		○ ○ ○ ○ ○	
○ ○ ○ ○ ○		○ ○ ○ ○ ○		○ ○ ○ ○ ○		○ ○ ○ ○ ○	

MARCH

MY MARCH INTENTIONS

The three things I am most looking forward to this month:

_____

_____

_____

The top three events that could prove expensive:

_____

_____

_____

My top three priorities at work, study or in family life:

_____

_____

_____

Three fun things I could do this month that are free:

_____

_____

_____

The top three people I want to connect with this month:

_____

_____

_____

This month will be a success if I can look back and know that:

_____

_____

_____

How I am currently feeling about my money:

MY MARCH SPENDING TRACKER

Date	Payment method	Expense	Category	Amount	Direct debit	Future Fund drawdown	Variable spending	Essential? Y/N	Entered?
				$.					○
				$.					○
				$.					○
				$.					○
				$.					○
				$.					○
				$.					○
				$.					○
				$.					○
				$.					○
				$.					○
				$.					○
				$.					○
				$.					○
				$.					○
				$.					○
				$.					○
				$.					○
				$.					○
				$.					○
				$.					○
				$.					○
				$.					○
				$.					○
				$.					○
				$.					○
				$.					○
				$.					○

Date	Payment method	Expense	Category	Amount	Direct debit	Future Fund drawdown	Variable spending	Essential? Y/N	Entered?
				$.					○
				$.					○
				$.					○
				$.					○
				$.					○
				$.					○
				$.					○
				$.					○
				$.					○
				$.					○
				$.					○
				$.					○
				$.					○
				$.					○
				$.					○
				$.					○
				$.					○
				$.					○
				$.					○
				$.					○
				$.					○
				$.					○
				$.					○
				$.					○
				$.					○
				$.					○
				$.					○
				$.					○
				$.					○
				$.					○
				$.					○
				$.					○
				$.					○

Date	Payment method	Expense	Category	Amount		Direct debit	Future Fund drawdown	Variable spending	Essential? Y/N	Entered?
				$	.					○
				$	.					○
				$	.					○
				$	.					○
				$	.					○
				$	.					○
				$	.					○
				$	.					○
				$	.					○
				$	.					○
				$	.					○
				$	.					○
				$	.					○
				$	.					○
				$	.					○
				$	.					○
				$	.					○
				$	.					○
				$	.					○
				$	.					○
				$	.					○
				$	.					○
				$	.					○
				$	.					○
				$	.					○
				$	.					○
				$	.					○
				$	.					○
				$	.					○
				$	.					○
				$	.					○
				$	.					○

Date	Payment method	Expense	Category	Amount	Direct debit	Future Fund drawdown	Variable spending	Essential? Y/N	Entered?
				$.					○
				$.					○
				$.					○
				$.					○
				$.					○
				$.					○
				$.					○
				$.					○
				$.					○
				$.					○
				$.					○
				$.					○
				$.					○
				$.					○
				$.					○
				$.					○
				$.					○
				$.					○
				$.					○
				$.					○
				$.					○
				$.					○
				$.					○
				$.					○
				$.					○
				$.					○
				$.					○
				$.					○
				$.					○
				$.					○
				$.					○
				$.					○

Date	Payment method	Expense	Category	Amount	Direct debit	Future Fund drawdown	Variable spending	Essential? Y/N	Entered?
				$.					○
				$.					○
				$.					○
				$.					○
				$.					○
				$.					○
				$.					○
				$.					○
				$.					○
				$.					○
				$.					○
				$.					○
				$.					○
				$.					○
				$.					○
				$.					○
				$.					○
				$.					○
				$.					○
				$.					○
				$.					○
				$.					○
				$.					○
				$.					○
				$.					○
				$.					○
				$.					○
				$.					○
				$.					○
				$.					○
				$.					○

MY MARCH BUDGET SUMMARY

INCOME

	$.		$.
	$.		$.

EXPENSES

Direct debits	Amount	Variable spending	Amount
	$.		$.
	$.		$.
	$.		$.
	$.		$.
	$.		$.
	$.		$.
	$.		$.
	$.		$.
	$.		$.
	$.		$.
Total direct debits	$.		$.
			$.

Future Fund contributions	Amount		
	$.		$.
	$.		$.
	$.		$.
	$.		$.
	$.		$.
	$.		$.
	$.		$.
	$.		$.
	$.		$.
Total Future Fund contributions	$.	**Total variable spending**	$.

TOTAL INCOME	$.	What I will do with this surplus	Amount
			$.
TOTAL EXPENSES	$.		$.
			$.
AMOUNT LEFT	$.		$.

MY MARCH REFLECTIONS

The three best things that happened to me this month:

....

....

....

The three purchases that brought me the most joy:

....

....

....

My top three achievements at work or study:

....

....

....

The three things I bought that, in hindsight, didn't bring much pleasure:

....

....

....

MONEY MINDMAP CHECK-IN

A negative thought about money I noticed this month was:

....

This thought made me feel: .... (refer to the emotions wheel)

Instead, I choose to flip this thought around and to think that:

....

How I am currently feeling about my money:

MY MARCH CHECKLIST

I am proud to say that this month I successfully (tick as appropriate):

☐ Recorded every dollar I spent in my spending tracker

☐ Created a monthly summary of my income and expenses

☐ Calculated my monthly surplus or deficit

☐ If in surplus, I decided how to allocate my surplus funds between paying off debt, increasing my cash buffer or investing and I have completed any transfers of funds or purchases required to implement those decisions

☐ If using them, I updated my Future Fund worksheets to reflect my monthly contributions and spending drawdowns

☐ Filled out my monthly spending totals on my annual tally sheet on page 210 of this diary

☐ Completed this month's Jess' challenge

☐ Reminded myself that I am not perfect, but am committed to making small changes to improve my finances

APRIL

My money, my choice

Jess' APRIL CHALLENGE

The changing of the seasons can prompt a spending spree on new clothing. Make the time to explore an op shop this month and buy something pre-loved.

☐ **Challenge accepted**

HABIT TRACKER

○ **Habit 1**

○ **Habit 2**

○ **Habit 3**

○ **Habit 4**

○ **Habit 5**

MONDAY	TUESDAY	WEDNESDAY

THURSDAY	FRIDAY	SATURDAY	SUNDAY
○ ○ ○ ○ ○	○ ○ ○ ○ ○	○ ○ ○ ○ ○	○ ○ ○ ○ ○
○ ○ ○ ○ ○	○ ○ ○ ○ ○	○ ○ ○ ○ ○	○ ○ ○ ○ ○
○ ○ ○ ○ ○	○ ○ ○ ○ ○	○ ○ ○ ○ ○	○ ○ ○ ○ ○
○ ○ ○ ○ ○	○ ○ ○ ○ ○	○ ○ ○ ○ ○	○ ○ ○ ○ ○
○ ○ ○ ○ ○	○ ○ ○ ○ ○	○ ○ ○ ○ ○	○ ○ ○ ○ ○

MY APRIL INTENTIONS

The three things I am most looking forward to this month:

....

....

....

The top three events that could prove expensive:

....

....

....

My top three priorities at work, study or in family life:

....

....

....

Three fun things I could do this month that are free:

....

....

....

The top three people I want to connect with this month:

....

....

....

This month will be a success if I can look back and know that:

....

....

....

How I am currently feeling about my money:

MY APRIL SPENDING TRACKER

Date	Payment method	Expense	Category	Amount	Direct debit	Future Fund drawdown	Variable spending	Essential? Y/N	Entered?
				$.					○
				$.					○
				$.					○
				$.					○
				$.					○
				$.					○
				$.					○
				$.					○
				$.					○
				$.					○
				$.					○
				$.					○
				$.					○
				$.					○
				$.					○
				$.					○
				$.					○
				$.					○
				$.					○
				$.					○
				$.					○
				$.					○
				$.					○
				$.					○
				$.					○
				$.					○
				$.					○
				$.					○
				$.					○
				$.					○
				$.					○

Date	Payment method	Expense	Category	Amount	Direct debit	Future Fund drawdown	Variable spending	Essential? Y/N	Entered?
				$.					○
				$.					○
				$.					○
				$.					○
				$.					○
				$.					○
				$.					○
				$.					○
				$.					○
				$.					○
				$.					○
				$.					○
				$.					○
				$.					○
				$.					○
				$.					○
				$.					○
				$.					○
				$.					○
				$.					○
				$.					○
				$.					○
				$.					○
				$.					○
				$.					○
				$.					○
				$.					○
				$.					○
				$.					○
				$.					○
				$.					○
				$.					○

Date	Payment method	Expense	Category	Amount		Direct debit	Future Fund drawdown	Variable spending	Essential? Y/N	Entered?
				$	.					◯
				$	.					◯
				$	.					◯
				$	.					◯
				$	.					◯
				$	.					◯
				$	.					◯
				$	.					◯
				$	.					◯
				$	.					◯
				$	.					◯
				$	.					◯
				$	.					◯
				$	.					◯
				$	.					◯
				$	.					◯
				$	.					◯
				$	.					◯
				$	.					◯
				$	.					◯
				$	.					◯
				$	.					◯
				$	.					◯
				$	.					◯
				$	.					◯
				$	.					◯
				$	.					◯
				$	.					◯
				$	.					◯
				$	.					◯
				$	.					◯
				$	.					◯

Date	Payment method	Expense	Category	Amount	Direct debit	Future Fund drawdown	Variable spending	Essential? Y/N	Entered?
				$.					○
				$.					○
				$.					○
				$.					○
				$.					○
				$.					○
				$.					○
				$.					○
				$.					○
				$.					○
				$.					○
				$.					○
				$.					○
				$.					○
				$.					○
				$.					○
				$.					○
				$.					○
				$.					○
				$.					○
				$.					○
				$.					○
				$.					○
				$.					○
				$.					○
				$.					○
				$.					○
				$.					○
				$.					○
				$.					○
				$.					○
				$.					○

Date	Payment method	Expense	Category	Amount	Direct debit	Future Fund drawdown	Variable spending	Essential? Y/N	Entered?
				$.					○
				$.					○
				$.					○
				$.					○
				$.					○
				$.					○
				$.					○
				$.					○
				$.					○
				$.					○
				$.					○
				$.					○
				$.					○
				$.					○
				$.					○
				$.					○
				$.					○
				$.					○
				$.					○
				$.					○
				$.					○
				$.					○
				$.					○
				$.					○
				$.					○
				$.					○
				$.					○
				$.					○
				$.					○
				$.					○
				$.					○
				$.					○

MY APRIL BUDGET SUMMARY

INCOME

	$.		$.
	$.		$.

EXPENSES

Direct debits	Amount	Variable spending	Amount
	$.		$.
	$.		$.
	$.		$.
	$.		$.
	$.		$.
	$.		$.
	$.		$.
	$.		$.
	$.		$.
	$.		$.
Total direct debits	$.		$.
			$.

Future Fund contributions	Amount		
	$.		$.
	$.		$.
	$.		$.
	$.		$.
	$.		$.
	$.		$.
	$.		$.
	$.		$.
	$.		$.
Total Future Fund contributions	$.	**Total variable spending**	$.

TOTAL INCOME	$.		

What I will do with this surplus	Amount
	$.
	$.
	$.
	$.

TOTAL EXPENSES	$.
AMOUNT LEFT	$.

MY APRIL REFLECTIONS

The three best things that happened to me this month:

....

....

....

The three purchases that brought me the most joy:

....

....

....

My top three achievements at work or study:

....

....

....

The three things I bought that, in hindsight, didn't bring much pleasure:

....

....

....

MONEY MINDMAP CHECK-IN

A negative thought about money I noticed this month was:

....

This thought made me feel: .... (refer to the emotions wheel)

Instead, I choose to flip this thought around and to think that:

....

How I am currently feeling about my money:

MY APRIL CHECKLIST

I am proud to say that this month I successfully (tick as appropriate):

☐ Recorded every dollar I spent in my spending tracker

☐ Created a monthly summary of my income and expenses

☐ Calculated my monthly surplus or deficit

☐ If in surplus, I decided how to allocate my surplus funds between paying off debt, increasing my cash buffer or investing and I have completed any transfers of funds or purchases required to implement those decisions

☐ If using them, I updated my Future Fund worksheets to reflect my monthly contributions and spending drawdowns

☐ Filled out my monthly spending totals on my annual tally sheet on page 210 of this diary

☐ Completed this month's Jess' challenge

☐ Reminded myself that I am not perfect, but am committed to making small changes to improve my finances

MAY

*How you spend your money is how
you spend your life*

	MONDAY		TUESDAY		WEDNESDAY	

Jess' MAY CHALLENGE

Did you know food is the second biggest expense in most household budgets after housing? Dial in your food costs by packing a home lunch to take to work each day this month.

☐ **Challenge accepted**

HABIT TRACKER

○ **Habit 1**

○ **Habit 2**

○ **Habit 3**

○ **Habit 4**

○ **Habit 5**

THURSDAY	FRIDAY	SATURDAY	SUNDAY

MY MAY INTENTIONS

The three things I am most looking forward to this month:

....

....

....

The top three events that could prove expensive:

....

....

....

My top three priorities at work, study or in family life:

....

....

....

Three fun things I could do this month that are free:

....

....

....

The top three people I want to connect with this month:

....

....

....

This month will be a success if I can look back and know that:

....

....

....

How I am currently feeling about my money:

MAY

MY MAY SPENDING TRACKER

Date	Payment method	Expense	Category	Amount	Direct debit	Future Fund drawdown	Variable spending	Essential? Y/N	Entered?
				$.					○
				$.					○
				$.					○
				$.					○
				$.					○
				$.					○
				$.					○
				$.					○
				$.					○
				$.					○
				$.					○
				$.					○
				$.					○
				$.					○
				$.					○
				$.					○
				$.					○
				$.					○
				$.					○
				$.					○
				$.					○
				$.					○
				$.					○
				$.					○
				$.					○
				$.					○
				$.					○
				$.					○
				$.					○

Date	Payment method	Expense	Category	Amount	Direct debit	Future Fund drawdown	Variable spending	Essential? Y/N	Entered?
				$.					○
				$.					○
				$.					○
				$.					○
				$.					○
				$.					○
				$.					○
				$.					○
				$.					○
				$.					○
				$.					○
				$.					○
				$.					○
				$.					○
				$.					○
				$.					○
				$.					○
				$.					○
				$.					○
				$.					○
				$.					○
				$.					○
				$.					○
				$.					○
				$.					○
				$.					○
				$.					○
				$.					○
				$.					○
				$.					○
				$.					○
				$.					○
				$.					○
				$.					○

Date	Payment method	Expense	Category	Amount	Direct debit	Future Fund drawdown	Variable spending	Essential? Y/N	Entered?
				$.					○
				$.					○
				$.					○
				$.					○
				$.					○
				$.					○
				$.					○
				$.					○
				$.					○
				$.					○
				$.					○
				$.					○
				$.					○
				$.					○
				$.					○
				$.					○
				$.					○
				$.					○
				$.					○
				$.					○
				$.					○
				$.					○
				$.					○
				$.					○
				$.					○
				$.					○
				$.					○
				$.					○
				$.					○
				$.					○
				$.					○
				$.					○

Date	Payment method	Expense	Category	Amount	Direct debit	Future Fund drawdown	Variable spending	Essential? Y/N	Entered?
				$.					○
				$.					○
				$.					○
				$.					○
				$.					○
				$.					○
				$.					○
				$.					○
				$.					○
				$.					○
				$.					○
				$.					○
				$.					○
				$.					○
				$.					○
				$.					○
				$.					○
				$.					○
				$.					○
				$.					○
				$.					○
				$.					○
				$.					○
				$.					○
				$.					○
				$.					○
				$.					○
				$.					○
				$.					○
				$.					○
				$.					○
				$.					○
				$.					○
				$.					○

Date	Payment method	Expense	Category	Amount	Direct debit	Future Fund drawdown	Variable spending	Essential? Y/N	Entered?
				$.					◯
				$.					◯
				$.					◯
				$.					◯
				$.					◯
				$.					◯
				$.					◯
				$.					◯
				$.					◯
				$.					◯
				$.					◯
				$.					◯
				$.					◯
				$.					◯
				$.					◯
				$.					◯
				$.					◯
				$.					◯
				$.					◯
				$.					◯
				$.					◯
				$.					◯
				$.					◯
				$.					◯
				$.					◯
				$.					◯
				$.					◯
				$.					◯
				$.					◯
				$.					◯

MY MAY BUDGET SUMMARY

INCOME			
	$.		$.
	$.		$.

EXPENSES

Direct debits	Amount	Variable spending	Amount
	$.		$.
	$.		$.
	$.		$.
	$.		$.
	$.		$.
	$.		$.
	$.		$.
	$.		$.
	$.		$.
Total direct debits	$.		$.
			$.
Future Fund contributions	**Amount**		$.
	$.		$.
	$.		$.
	$.		$.
	$.		$.
	$.		$.
	$.		$.
	$.		$.
	$.		$.
Total Future Fund contributions	$.	**Total variable spending**	$.

TOTAL INCOME	$.	What I will do with this surplus	Amount
			$.
TOTAL EXPENSES	$.		$.
			$.
AMOUNT LEFT	$.		$.

MY MAY REFLECTIONS

The three best things that happened to me this month:

....

....

....

The three purchases that brought me the most joy:

....

....

....

My top three achievements at work or study:

....

....

....

The three things I bought that, in hindsight, didn't bring much pleasure:

....

....

....

MONEY MINDMAP CHECK-IN

A negative thought about money I noticed this month was:

....

This thought made me feel: .... (refer to the emotions wheel)

Instead, I choose to flip this thought around and to think that:

....

How I am currently feeling about my money:

MY MAY CHECKLIST

I am proud to say that this month I successfully (tick as appropriate):

- ☐ Recorded every dollar I spent in my spending tracker

- ☐ Created a monthly summary of my income and expenses

- ☐ Calculated my monthly surplus or deficit

- ☐ If in surplus, I decided how to allocate my surplus funds between paying off debt, increasing my cash buffer or investing and I have completed any transfers of funds or purchases required to implement those decisions

- ☐ If using them, I updated my Future Fund worksheets to reflect my monthly contributions and spending drawdowns

- ☐ Filled out my monthly spending totals on my annual tally sheet on page 210 of this diary

- ☐ Completed this month's Jess' challenge

- ☐ Reminded myself that I am not perfect, but am committed to making small changes to improve my finances

JUNE

You are not weird.
You are excellent!

Jess' JUNE CHALLENGE

Cancel a streaming service this month! Instead, watch free-to-air or catch-up TV services, while also trialling the free introductory offers of alternative providers.

☐ **Challenge accepted**

HABIT TRACKER

○ **Habit 1**

○ **Habit 2**

○ **Habit 3**

○ **Habit 4**

○ **Habit 5**

MONDAY	TUESDAY	WEDNESDAY

THURSDAY		FRIDAY		SATURDAY		SUNDAY	
	○		○		○		○
	○		○		○		○
	○		○		○		○
	○		○		○		○
	○		○		○		○
	○		○		○		○
	○		○		○		○
	○		○		○		○
	○		○		○		○
	○		○		○		○
	○		○		○		○
	○		○		○		○
	○		○		○		○
	○		○		○		○
	○		○		○		○
	○		○		○		○
	○		○		○		○
	○		○		○		○
	○		○		○		○
	○		○		○		○
	○		○		○		○
	○		○		○		○
	○		○		○		○
	○		○		○		○
	○		○		○		○

MY JUNE INTENTIONS

JUNE

The three things I am most looking forward to this month:

....

....

....

The top three events that could prove expensive:

....

....

....

My top three priorities at work, study or in family life:

....

....

....

Three fun things I could do this month that are free:

....

....

....

The top three people I want to connect with this month:

....

....

....

This month will be a success if I can look back and know that:

....

....

....

How I am currently feeling about my money:

MY JUNE SPENDING TRACKER

Date	Payment method	Expense	Category	Amount	Direct debit	Future Fund drawdown	Variable spending	Essential? Y/N	Entered?
				$.					◯
				$.					◯
				$.					◯
				$.					◯
				$.					◯
				$.					◯
				$.					◯
				$.					◯
				$.					◯
				$.					◯
				$.					◯
				$.					◯
				$.					◯
				$.					◯
				$.					◯
				$.					◯
				$.					◯
				$.					◯
				$.					◯
				$.					◯
				$.					◯
				$.					◯
				$.					◯
				$.					◯
				$.					◯
				$.					◯
				$.					◯
				$.					◯

Date	Payment method	Expense	Category	Amount	Direct debit	Future Fund drawdown	Variable spending	Essential? Y/N	Entered?
				$.					○
				$.					○
				$.					○
				$.					○
				$.					○
				$.					○
				$.					○
				$.					○
				$.					○
				$.					○
				$.					○
				$.					○
				$.					○
				$.					○
				$.					○
				$.					○
				$.					○
				$.					○
				$.					○
				$.					○
				$.					○
				$.					○
				$.					○
				$.					○
				$.					○
				$.					○
				$.					○
				$.					○
				$.					○
				$.					○
				$.					○
				$.					○
				$.					○

Date	Payment method	Expense	Category	Amount	Direct debit	Future Fund drawdown	Variable spending	Essential? Y/N	Entered?
				$.					○
				$.					○
				$.					○
				$.					○
				$.					○
				$.					○
				$.					○
				$.					○
				$.					○
				$.					○
				$.					○
				$.					○
				$.					○
				$.					○
				$.					○
				$.					○
				$.					○
				$.					○
				$.					○
				$.					○
				$.					○
				$.					○
				$.					○
				$.					○
				$.					○
				$.					○
				$.					○
				$.					○
				$.					○
				$.					○

Date	Payment method	Expense	Category	Amount	Direct debit	Future Fund drawdown	Variable spending	Essential? Y/N	Entered?
				$.					○
				$.					○
				$.					○
				$.					○
				$.					○
				$.					○
				$.					○
				$.					○
				$.					○
				$.					○
				$.					○
				$.					○
				$.					○
				$.					○
				$.					○
				$.					○
				$.					○
				$.					○
				$.					○
				$.					○
				$.					○
				$.					○
				$.					○
				$.					○
				$.					○
				$.					○
				$.					○
				$.					○
				$.					○
				$.					○
				$.					○
				$.					○

Date	Payment method	Expense	Category	Amount		Direct debit	Future Fund drawdown	Variable spending	Essential? Y/N	Entered?
				$	.					○
				$	.					○
				$	.					○
				$	.					○
				$	.					○
				$	.					○
				$	.					○
				$	.					○
				$	.					○
				$	.					○
				$	.					○
				$	.					○
				$	.					○
				$	.					○
				$	.					○
				$	.					○
				$	.					○
				$	.					○
				$	.					○
				$	.					○
				$	.					○
				$	.					○
				$	.					○
				$	.					○
				$	.					○
				$	.					○
				$	.					○
				$	.					○
				$	.					○
				$	.					○
				$	.					○

MY JUNE BUDGET SUMMARY

INCOME

	$.		$.
	$.		$.

EXPENSES

Direct debits	Amount	Variable spending	Amount
	$.		$.
	$.		$.
	$.		$.
	$.		$.
	$.		$.
	$.		$.
	$.		$.
	$.		$.
	$.		$.
Total direct debits	$.		$.
			$.

Future Fund contributions	Amount		$.
	$.		$.
	$.		$.
	$.		$.
	$.		$.
	$.		$.
	$.		$.
	$.		$.
	$.		$.
	$.		$.
Total Future Fund contributions	$.	**Total variable spending**	$.

TOTAL INCOME	$.	What I will do with this surplus	Amount
			$.
TOTAL EXPENSES	$.		$.
			$.
AMOUNT LEFT	$.		$.

MY JUNE REFLECTIONS

The three best things that happened to me this month:

....

....

....

The three purchases that brought me the most joy:

....

....

....

My top three achievements at work or study:

....

....

....

The three things I bought that, in hindsight, didn't bring much pleasure:

....

....

....

MONEY MINDMAP CHECK-IN

A negative thought about money I noticed this month was:

....

This thought made me feel: .... (refer to the emotions wheel)

Instead, I choose to flip this thought around and to think that:

....

How I am currently feeling about my money:

MY JUNE CHECKLIST

I am proud to say that this month I successfully (tick as appropriate):

- ☐ Recorded every dollar I spent in my spending tracker

- ☐ Created a monthly summary of my income and expenses

- ☐ Calculated my monthly surplus or deficit

- ☐ If in surplus, I decided how to allocate my surplus funds between paying off debt, increasing my cash buffer or investing and I have completed any transfers of funds or purchases required to implement those decisions

- ☐ If using them, I updated my Future Fund worksheets to reflect my monthly contributions and spending drawdowns

- ☐ Filled out my monthly spending totals on my annual tally sheet on page 210 of this diary

- ☐ Completed this month's Jess' challenge

- ☐ Reminded myself that I am not perfect, but am committed to making small changes to improve my finances

JULY

Spend less than you earn; invest the rest

	MONDAY		TUESDAY		WEDNESDAY	

Jess' JULY CHALLENGE

Alcohol can be a large hidden cost in many household budgets. Opting to participate in a 'Dry July' this month can bring a host of benefits, including cutting costs.

☐ **Challenge accepted**

HABIT TRACKER

○ **Habit 1**

○ **Habit 2**

○ **Habit 3**

○ **Habit 4**

○ **Habit 5**

THURSDAY	FRIDAY	SATURDAY	SUNDAY

MY JULY INTENTIONS

JULY

The three things I am most looking forward to this month:

The top three events that could prove expensive:

My top three priorities at work, study or in family life:

Three fun things I could do this month that are free:

The top three people I want to connect with this month:

This month will be a success if I can look back and know that:

How I am currently feeling about my money:

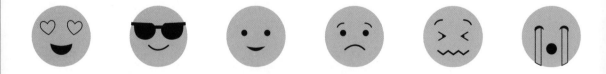

MY JULY SPENDING TRACKER

Date	Payment method	Expense	Category	Amount	Direct debit	Future Fund drawdown	Variable spending	Essential? Y/N	Entered?
				$.					○
				$.					○
				$.					○
				$.					○
				$.					○
				$.					○
				$.					○
				$.					○
				$.					○
				$.					○
				$.					○
				$.					○
				$.					○
				$.					○
				$.					○
				$.					○
				$.					○
				$.					○
				$.					○
				$.					○
				$.					○
				$.					○
				$.					○
				$.					○
				$.					○
				$.					○
				$.					○
				$.					○
				$.					○

Date	Payment method	Expense	Category	Amount	Direct debit	Future Fund drawdown	Variable spending	Essential? Y/N	Entered?
				$.					◯
				$.					◯
				$.					◯
				$.					◯
				$.					◯
				$.					◯
				$.					◯
				$.					◯
				$.					◯
				$.					◯
				$.					◯
				$.					◯
				$.					◯
				$.					◯
				$.					◯
				$.					◯
				$.					◯
				$.					◯
				$.					◯
				$.					◯
				$.					◯
				$.					◯
				$.					◯
				$.					◯
				$.					◯
				$.					◯
				$.					◯
				$.					◯
				$.					◯
				$.					◯
				$.					◯
				$.					◯

Date	Payment method	Expense	Category	Amount	Direct debit	Future Fund drawdown	Variable spending	Essential? Y/N	Entered?
				$.					○
				$.					○
				$.					○
				$.					○
				$.					○
				$.					○
				$.					○
				$.					○
				$.					○
				$.					○
				$.					○
				$.					○
				$.					○
				$.					○
				$.					○
				$.					○
				$.					○
				$.					○
				$.					○
				$.					○
				$.					○
				$.					○
				$.					○
				$.					○
				$.					○
				$.					○
				$.					○
				$.					○
				$.					○
				$.					○

Date	Payment method	Expense	Category	Amount	Direct debit	Future Fund drawdown	Variable spending	Essential? Y/N	Entered?
				$.					○
				$.					○
				$.					○
				$.					○
				$.					○
				$.					○
				$.					○
				$.					○
				$.					○
				$.					○
				$.					○
				$.					○
				$.					○
				$.					○
				$.					○
				$.					○
				$.					○
				$.					○
				$.					○
				$.					○
				$.					○
				$.					○
				$.					○
				$.					○
				$.					○
				$.					○
				$.					○
				$.					○
				$.					○
				$.					○
				$.					○
				$.					○
				$.					○
				$.					○

Date	Payment method	Expense	Category	Amount	Direct debit	Future Fund drawdown	Variable spending	Essential? Y/N	Entered?
				$.					○
				$.					○
				$.					○
				$.					○
				$.					○
				$.					○
				$.					○
				$.					○
				$.					○
				$.					○
				$.					○
				$.					○
				$.					○
				$.					○
				$.					○
				$.					○
				$.					○
				$.					○
				$.					○
				$.					○
				$.					○
				$.					○
				$.					○
				$.					○
				$.					○
				$.					○
				$.					○
				$.					○
				$.					○
				$.					○
				$.					○
				$.					○

JULY

MY JULY BUDGET SUMMARY

INCOME

	$.		$.
	$.		$.

EXPENSES

Direct debits	Amount	Variable spending	Amount
	$.		$.
	$.		$.
	$.		$.
	$.		$.
	$.		$.
	$.		$.
	$.		$.
	$.		$.
	$.		$.
Total direct debits	$.		$.
			$.

Future Fund contributions	Amount		
	$.		$.
	$.		$.
	$.		$.
	$.		$.
	$.		$.
	$.		$.
	$.		$.
	$.		$.
	$.		$.
Total Future Fund contributions	$.	**Total variable spending**	$.

		What I will do with this surplus	Amount
TOTAL INCOME	$.		$.
			$.
TOTAL EXPENSES	$.		$.
			$.
AMOUNT LEFT	$.		$.

MY JULY REFLECTIONS

The three best things that happened to me this month:

....

....

....

The three purchases that brought me the most joy:

....

....

....

My top three achievements at work or study:

....

....

....

The three things I bought that, in hindsight, didn't bring much pleasure:

....

....

....

MONEY MINDMAP CHECK-IN

A negative thought about money I noticed this month was:

....

This thought made me feel: .... (refer to the emotions wheel)

Instead, I choose to flip this thought around and to think that:

....

How I am currently feeling about my money:

MY JULY CHECKLIST

I am proud to say that this month I successfully (tick as appropriate):

- ☐ Recorded every dollar I spent in my spending tracker

- ☐ Created a monthly summary of my income and expenses

- ☐ Calculated my monthly surplus or deficit

- ☐ If in surplus, I decided how to allocate my surplus funds between paying off debt, increasing my cash buffer or investing and I have completed any transfers of funds or purchases required to implement those decisions

- ☐ If using them, I updated my Future Fund worksheets to reflect my monthly contributions and spending drawdowns

- ☐ Filled out my monthly spending totals on my annual tally sheet on page 210 of this diary

- ☐ Completed this month's Jess' challenge

- ☐ Reminded myself that I am not perfect, but am committed to making small changes to improve my finances

AUGUST

Money is not a measure of
your worth

Jess' AUGUST CHALLENGE

	MONDAY		TUESDAY		WEDNESDAY	

Try a side hustle! Whether it's selling your stuff, dog walking, freelance writing, babysitting, market surveys or renting out a room or car space, google 'side hustle ideas' and get inspired.

☐ **Challenge accepted**

HABIT TRACKER

○ **Habit 1**

○ **Habit 2**

○ **Habit 3**

○ **Habit 4**

○ **Habit 5**

THURSDAY	FRIDAY	SATURDAY	SUNDAY

MY AUGUST INTENTIONS

The three things I am most looking forward to this month:

_____

_____

_____

The top three events that could prove expensive:

_____

_____

_____

My top three priorities at work, study or in family life:

_____

_____

_____

Three fun things I could do this month that are free:

_____

_____

_____

The top three people I want to connect with this month:

_____

_____

_____

This month will be a success if I can look back and know that:

_____

_____

_____

How I am currently feeling about my money:

MY AUGUST SPENDING TRACKER

Date	Payment method	Expense	Category	Amount	Direct debit	Future Fund drawdown	Variable spending	Essential? Y/N	Entered?
				$.					○
				$.					○
				$.					○
				$.					○
				$.					○
				$.					○
				$.					○
				$.					○
				$.					○
				$.					○
				$.					○
				$.					○
				$.					○
				$.					○
				$.					○
				$.					○
				$.					○
				$.					○
				$.					○
				$.					○
				$.					○
				$.					○
				$.					○
				$.					○
				$.					○
				$.					○
				$.					○
				$.					○

Date	Payment method	Expense	Category	Amount	Direct debit	Future Fund drawdown	Variable spending	Essential? Y/N	Entered?
				$.					◯
				$.					◯
				$.					◯
				$.					◯
				$.					◯
				$.					◯
				$.					◯
				$.					◯
				$.					◯
				$.					◯
				$.					◯
				$.					◯
				$.					◯
				$.					◯
				$.					◯
				$.					◯
				$.					◯
				$.					◯
				$.					◯
				$.					◯
				$.					◯
				$.					◯
				$.					◯
				$.					◯
				$.					◯
				$.					◯
				$.					◯
				$.					◯
				$.					◯
				$.					◯
				$.					◯

Date	Payment method	Expense	Category	Amount	Direct debit	Future Fund drawdown	Variable spending	Essential? Y/N	Entered?
				$.					◯
				$.					◯
				$.					◯
				$.					◯
				$.					◯
				$.					◯
				$.					◯
				$.					◯
				$.					◯
				$.					◯
				$.					◯
				$.					◯
				$.					◯
				$.					◯
				$.					◯
				$.					◯
				$.					◯
				$.					◯
				$.					◯
				$.					◯
				$.					◯
				$.					◯
				$.					◯
				$.					◯
				$.					◯
				$.					◯
				$.					◯
				$.					◯
				$.					◯
				$.					◯
				$.					◯
				$.					◯
				$.					◯
				$.					◯

Date	Payment method	Expense	Category	Amount	Direct debit	Future Fund drawdown	Variable spending	Essential? Y/N	Entered?
				$.					○
				$.					○
				$.					○
				$.					○
				$.					○
				$.					○
				$.					○
				$.					○
				$.					○
				$.					○
				$.					○
				$.					○
				$.					○
				$.					○
				$.					○
				$.					○
				$.					○
				$.					○
				$.					○
				$.					○
				$.					○
				$.					○
				$.					○
				$.					○
				$.					○
				$.					○
				$.					○
				$.					○
				$.					○
				$.					○
				$.					○
				$.					○

Date	Payment method	Expense	Category	Amount	Direct debit	Future Fund drawdown	Variable spending	Essential? Y/N	Entered?
				$.					○
				$.					○
				$.					○
				$.					○
				$.					○
				$.					○
				$.					○
				$.					○
				$.					○
				$.					○
				$.					○
				$.					○
				$.					○
				$.					○
				$.					○
				$.					○
				$.					○
				$.					○
				$.					○
				$.					○
				$.					○
				$.					○
				$.					○
				$.					○
				$.					○
				$.					○
				$.					○
				$.					○
				$.					○
				$.					○
				$.					○

AUGUST

MY AUGUST BUDGET SUMMARY

INCOME

	$.		$.
	$.		$.

EXPENSES

Direct debits	Amount	Variable spending	Amount
	$.		$.
	$.		$.
	$.		$.
	$.		$.
	$.		$.
	$.		$.
	$.		$.
	$.		$.
	$.		$.
	$.		$.
Total direct debits	$.		$.
			$.

Future Fund contributions	Amount		
	$.		$.
	$.		$.
	$.		$.
	$.		$.
	$.		$.
	$.		$.
	$.		$.
	$.		$.
	$.		$.
Total Future Fund contributions	$.	**Total variable spending**	$.

		What I will do with this surplus	Amount
TOTAL INCOME	$.		$.
TOTAL EXPENSES	$.		$.
			$.
AMOUNT LEFT	$.		$.

MY AUGUST REFLECTIONS

The three best things that happened to me this month:

....

....

....

The three purchases that brought me the most joy:

....

....

....

My top three achievements at work or study:

....

....

....

The three things I bought that, in hindsight, didn't bring much pleasure:

....

....

....

MONEY MINDMAP CHECK-IN

A negative thought about money I noticed this month was:

....

This thought made me feel: .... (refer to the emotions wheel)

Instead, I choose to flip this thought around and to think that:

....

How I am currently feeling about my money:

MY AUGUST CHECKLIST

I am proud to say that this month I successfully (tick as appropriate):

- ☐ Recorded every dollar I spent in my spending tracker

- ☐ Created a monthly summary of my income and expenses

- ☐ Calculated my monthly surplus or deficit

- ☐ If in surplus, I decided how to allocate my surplus funds between paying off debt, increasing my cash buffer or investing and I have completed any transfers of funds or purchases required to implement those decisions

- ☐ If using them, I updated my Future Fund worksheets to reflect my monthly contributions and spending drawdowns

- ☐ Filled out my monthly spending totals on my annual tally sheet on page 210 of this diary

- ☐ Completed this month's Jess' challenge

- ☐ Reminded myself that I am not perfect, but am committed to making small changes to improve my finances

SEPTEMBER

Money is just a tool. You get to control how you use it

	MONDAY	TUESDAY	WEDNESDAY

Jess'
SEPTEMBER CHALLENGE

Getting fit and healthy doesn't need to cost the world. Try a free online yoga YouTube video or download and try a free fitness app such as the Nike Training Club app.

☐ **Challenge accepted**

HABIT TRACKER

○ **Habit 1**

○ **Habit 2**

○ **Habit 3**

○ **Habit 4**

○ **Habit 5**

THURSDAY	FRIDAY	SATURDAY	SUNDAY

MY SEPTEMBER INTENTIONS

The three things I am most looking forward to this month:

_____

_____

_____

My top three priorities at work, study or in family life:

_____

_____

_____

The top three people I want to connect with this month:

_____

_____

_____

The top three events that could prove expensive:

_____

_____

_____

Three fun things I could do this month that are free:

_____

_____

_____

This month will be a success if I can look back and know that:

_____

_____

_____

How I am currently feeling about my money:

MY SEPTEMBER SPENDING TRACKER

Date	Payment method	Expense	Category	Amount	Direct debit	Future Fund drawdown	Variable spending	Essential? Y/N	Entered?
				$.					○
				$.					○
				$.					○
				$.					○
				$.					○
				$.					○
				$.					○
				$.					○
				$.					○
				$.					○
				$.					○
				$.					○
				$.					○
				$.					○
				$.					○
				$.					○
				$.					○
				$.					○
				$.					○
				$.					○
				$.					○
				$.					○
				$.					○
				$.					○
				$.					○
				$.					○
				$.					○
				$.					○
				$.					○
				$.					○

Date	Payment method	Expense	Category	Amount	Direct debit	Future Fund drawdown	Variable spending	Essential? Y/N	Entered?
				$.					○
				$.					○
				$.					○
				$.					○
				$.					○
				$.					○
				$.					○
				$.					○
				$.					○
				$.					○
				$.					○
				$.					○
				$.					○
				$.					○
				$.					○
				$.					○
				$.					○
				$.					○
				$.					○
				$.					○
				$.					○
				$.					○
				$.					○
				$.					○
				$.					○
				$.					○
				$.					○
				$.					○
				$.					○
				$.					○

Date	Payment method	Expense	Category	Amount	Direct debit	Future Fund drawdown	Variable spending	Essential? Y/N	Entered?
				$.					◯
				$.					◯
				$.					◯
				$.					◯
				$.					◯
				$.					◯
				$.					◯
				$.					◯
				$.					◯
				$.					◯
				$.					◯
				$.					◯
				$.					◯
				$.					◯
				$.					◯
				$.					◯
				$.					◯
				$.					◯
				$.					◯
				$.					◯
				$.					◯
				$.					◯
				$.					◯
				$.					◯
				$.					◯
				$.					◯
				$.					◯
				$.					◯
				$.					◯
				$.					◯
				$.					◯
				$.					◯
				$.					◯
				$.					◯
				$.					◯

Date	Payment method	Expense	Category	Amount	Direct debit	Future Fund drawdown	Variable spending	Essential? Y/N	Entered?
				$.					○
				$.					○
				$.					○
				$.					○
				$.					○
				$.					○
				$.					○
				$.					○
				$.					○
				$.					○
				$.					○
				$.					○
				$.					○
				$.					○
				$.					○
				$.					○
				$.					○
				$.					○
				$.					○
				$.					○
				$.					○
				$.					○
				$.					○
				$.					○
				$.					○
				$.					○
				$.					○
				$.					○
				$.					○
				$.					○

Date	Payment method	Expense	Category	Amount	Direct debit	Future Fund drawdown	Variable spending	Essential? Y/N	Entered?
				$.					○
				$.					○
				$.					○
				$.					○
				$.					○
				$.					○
				$.					○
				$.					○
				$.					○
				$.					○
				$.					○
				$.					○
				$.					○
				$.					○
				$.					○
				$.					○
				$.					○
				$.					○
				$.					○
				$.					○
				$.					○
				$.					○
				$.					○
				$.					○
				$.					○
				$.					○
				$.					○
				$.					○
				$.					○
				$.					○
				$.					○
				$.					○
				$.					○

MY SEPTEMBER BUDGET SUMMARY

INCOME

	$.		$.
	$.		$.

EXPENSES

Direct debits	Amount	Variable spending	Amount
	$.		$.
	$.		$.
	$.		$.
	$.		$.
	$.		$.
	$.		$.
	$.		$.
	$.		$.
	$.		$.
Total direct debits	$.		$.
			$.

Future Fund contributions	Amount		$.
	$.		$.
	$.		$.
	$.		$.
	$.		$.
	$.		$.
	$.		$.
	$.		$.
	$.		$.
Total Future Fund contributions	$.	**Total variable spending**	$.

TOTAL INCOME	$.	What I will do with this surplus	Amount
			$.
TOTAL EXPENSES	$.		$.
			$.
AMOUNT LEFT	$.		$.

SEPTEMBER

MY SEPTEMBER REFLECTIONS

The three best things that happened to me this month:

....

....

....

The three purchases that brought me the most joy:

....

....

....

My top three achievements at work or study:

....

....

....

The three things I bought that, in hindsight, didn't bring much pleasure:

....

....

....

MONEY MINDMAP CHECK-IN

A negative thought about money I noticed this month was:

....

This thought made me feel: .... (refer to the emotions wheel)

Instead, I choose to flip this thought around and to think that:

....

How I am currently feeling about my money:

MY SEPTEMBER CHECKLIST

I am proud to say that this month I successfully (tick as appropriate):

- ☐ Recorded every dollar I spent in my spending tracker

- ☐ Created a monthly summary of my income and expenses

- ☐ Calculated my monthly surplus or deficit

- ☐ If in surplus, I decided how to allocate my surplus funds between paying off debt, increasing my cash buffer or investing and I have completed any transfers of funds or purchases required to implement those decisions

- ☐ If using them, I updated my Future Fund worksheets to reflect my monthly contributions and spending drawdowns

- ☐ Filled out my monthly spending totals on my annual tally sheet on page 210 of this diary

- ☐ Completed this month's Jess' challenge

- ☐ Reminded myself that I am not perfect, but am committed to making small changes to improve my finances

OCTOBER

Money is freedom

Jess'
OCTOBER CHALLENGE

Insurances are a big cost in most budgets. Use a comparison site to review the pricing of one policy and switch or call your insurer for a better deal!

☐ **Challenge accepted**

HABIT TRACKER

○ **Habit 1**

○ **Habit 2**

○ **Habit 3**

○ **Habit 4**

○ **Habit 5**

MONDAY	TUESDAY	WEDNESDAY

THURSDAY		FRIDAY		SATURDAY		SUNDAY	
	○		○		○		○
	○		○		○		○
	○		○		○		○
	○		○		○		○
	○		○		○		○
	○		○		○		○
	○		○		○		○
	○		○		○		○
	○		○		○		○
	○		○		○		○
	○		○		○		○
	○		○		○		○
	○		○		○		○
	○		○		○		○
	○		○		○		○
	○		○		○		○
	○		○		○		○
	○		○		○		○
	○		○		○		○
	○		○		○		○
	○		○		○		○
	○		○		○		○
	○		○		○		○
	○		○		○		○
	○		○		○		○

MY OCTOBER INTENTIONS

The three things I am most looking forward to this month:

....

....

....

The top three events that could prove expensive:

....

....

....

My top three priorities at work, study or in family life:

....

....

....

Three fun things I could do this month that are free:

....

....

....

The top three people I want to connect with this month:

....

....

....

This month will be a success if I can look back and know that:

....

....

....

How I am currently feeling about my money:

MY OCTOBER SPENDING TRACKER

Date	Payment method	Expense	Category	Amount	Direct debit	Future Fund drawdown	Variable spending	Essential? Y/N	Entered?
				$.					◯
				$.					◯
				$.					◯
				$.					◯
				$.					◯
				$.					◯
				$.					◯
				$.					◯
				$.					◯
				$.					◯
				$.					◯
				$.					◯
				$.					◯
				$.					◯
				$.					◯
				$.					◯
				$.					◯
				$.					◯
				$.					◯
				$.					◯
				$.					◯
				$.					◯
				$.					◯
				$.					◯
				$.					◯
				$.					◯
				$.					◯
				$.					◯

Date	Payment method	Expense	Category	Amount	Direct debit	Future Fund drawdown	Variable spending	Essential? Y/N	Entered?
				$.					○
				$.					○
				$.					○
				$.					○
				$.					○
				$.					○
				$.					○
				$.					○
				$.					○
				$.					○
				$.					○
				$.					○
				$.					○
				$.					○
				$.					○
				$.					○
				$.					○
				$.					○
				$.					○
				$.					○
				$.					○
				$.					○
				$.					○
				$.					○
				$.					○
				$.					○
				$.					○
				$.					○
				$.					○
				$.					○
				$.					○
				$.					○

Date	Payment method	Expense	Category	Amount	Direct debit	Future Fund drawdown	Variable spending	Essential? Y/N	Entered?
				$.					○
				$.					○
				$.					○
				$.					○
				$.					○
				$.					○
				$.					○
				$.					○
				$.					○
				$.					○
				$.					○
				$.					○
				$.					○
				$.					○
				$.					○
				$.					○
				$.					○
				$.					○
				$.					○
				$.					○
				$.					○
				$.					○
				$.					○
				$.					○
				$.					○
				$.					○
				$.					○
				$.					○
				$.					○
				$.					○
				$.					○
				$.					○

OCTOBER

Date	Payment method	Expense	Category	Amount	Direct debit	Future Fund drawdown	Variable spending	Essential? Y/N	Entered?
				$.					○
				$.					○
				$.					○
				$.					○
				$.					○
				$.					○
				$.					○
				$.					○
				$.					○
				$.					○
				$.					○
				$.					○
				$.					○
				$.					○
				$.					○
				$.					○
				$.					○
				$.					○
				$.					○
				$.					○
				$.					○
				$.					○
				$.					○
				$.					○
				$.					○
				$.					○
				$.					○
				$.					○
				$.					○
				$.					○
				$.					○

Date	Payment method	Expense	Category	Amount	Direct debit	Future Fund drawdown	Variable spending	Essential? Y/N	Entered?
				$.					○
				$.					○
				$.					○
				$.					○
				$.					○
				$.					○
				$.					○
				$.					○
				$.					○
				$.					○
				$.					○
				$.					○
				$.					○
				$.					○
				$.					○
				$.					○
				$.					○
				$.					○
				$.					○
				$.					○
				$.					○
				$.					○
				$.					○
				$.					○
				$.					○
				$.					○
				$.					○
				$.					○
				$.					○
				$.					○
				$.					○
				$.					○

MY OCTOBER BUDGET SUMMARY

INCOME

	Amount		Amount
	$.		$.
	$.		$.

EXPENSES

Direct debits	Amount	Variable spending	Amount
	$.		$.
	$.		$.
	$.		$.
	$.		$.
	$.		$.
	$.		$.
	$.		$.
	$.		$.
	$.		$.
Total direct debits	$.		$.
			$.

Future Fund contributions	Amount		$.
	$.		$.
	$.		$.
	$.		$.
	$.		$.
	$.		$.
	$.		$.
	$.		$.
	$.		$.
	$.		$.
Total Future Fund contributions	$.	Total variable spending	$.

TOTAL INCOME	$.	What I will do with this surplus	Amount
			$.
TOTAL EXPENSES	$.		$.
			$.
AMOUNT LEFT	$.		$.

MY OCTOBER REFLECTIONS

The three best things that happened to me this month:

....

....

....

The three purchases that brought me the most joy:

....

....

....

My top three achievements at work or study:

....

....

....

The three things I bought that, in hindsight, didn't bring much pleasure:

....

....

....

MONEY MINDMAP CHECK-IN

A negative thought about money I noticed this month was:

....

This thought made me feel: .... (refer to the emotions wheel)

Instead, I choose to flip this thought around and to think that:

....

How I am currently feeling about my money:

MY OCTOBER CHECKLIST

I am proud to say that this month I successfully (tick as appropriate):

- ☐ Recorded every dollar I spent in my spending tracker

- ☐ Created a monthly summary of my income and expenses

- ☐ Calculated my monthly surplus or deficit

- ☐ If in surplus, I decided how to allocate my surplus funds between paying off debt, increasing my cash buffer or investing and I have completed any transfers of funds or purchases required to implement those decisions

- ☐ If using them, I updated my Future Fund worksheets to reflect my monthly contributions and spending drawdowns

- ☐ Filled out my monthly spending totals on my annual tally sheet on page 210 of this diary

- ☐ Completed this month's Jess' challenge

- ☐ Reminded myself that I am not perfect, but am committed to making small changes to improve my finances

NOVEMBER

It's okay to spend money on things that bring you joy. Just find your true joy first

Jess' NOVEMBER CHALLENGE	MONDAY		TUESDAY		WEDNESDAY	

Jess' NOVEMBER CHALLENGE

Set yourself up for a stress-free December by using online sales such as Black Friday and Cyber Monday to complete all your Christmas shopping by month's end. You can do it!

☐ **Challenge accepted**

HABIT TRACKER

○ **Habit 1**

○ **Habit 2**

○ **Habit 3**

○ **Habit 4**

○ **Habit 5**

THURSDAY	FRIDAY	SATURDAY	SUNDAY

MY NOVEMBER INTENTIONS

The three things I am most looking forward to this month:

....

....

....

The top three events that could prove expensive:

....

....

....

My top three priorities at work, study or in family life:

....

....

....

Three fun things I could do this month that are free:

....

....

....

The top three people I want to connect with this month:

....

....

....

This month will be a success if I can look back and know that:

....

....

....

How I am currently feeling about my money:

MY NOVEMBER SPENDING TRACKER

Date	Payment method	Expense	Category	Amount	Direct debit	Future Fund drawdown	Variable spending	Essential? Y/N	Entered?
				$.					○
				$.					○
				$.					○
				$.					○
				$.					○
				$.					○
				$.					○
				$.					○
				$.					○
				$.					○
				$.					○
				$.					○
				$.					○
				$.					○
				$.					○
				$.					○
				$.					○
				$.					○
				$.					○
				$.					○
				$.					○
				$.					○
				$.					○
				$.					○
				$.					○
				$.					○
				$.					○
				$.					○
				$.					○

Date	Payment method	Expense	Category	Amount	Direct debit	Future Fund drawdown	Variable spending	Essential? Y/N	Entered?
				$.					◯
				$.					◯
				$.					◯
				$.					◯
				$.					◯
				$.					◯
				$.					◯
				$.					◯
				$.					◯
				$.					◯
				$.					◯
				$.					◯
				$.					◯
				$.					◯
				$.					◯
				$.					◯
				$.					◯
				$.					◯
				$.					◯
				$.					◯
				$.					◯
				$.					◯
				$.					◯
				$.					◯
				$.					◯
				$.					◯
				$.					◯
				$.					◯
				$.					◯
				$.					◯
				$.					◯
				$.					◯

Date	Payment method	Expense	Category	Amount	Direct debit	Future Fund drawdown	Variable spending	Essential? Y/N	Entered?
				$.					◯
				$.					◯
				$.					◯
				$.					◯
				$.					◯
				$.					◯
				$.					◯
				$.					◯
				$.					◯
				$.					◯
				$.					◯
				$.					◯
				$.					◯
				$.					◯
				$.					◯
				$.					◯
				$.					◯
				$.					◯
				$.					◯
				$.					◯
				$.					◯
				$.					◯
				$.					◯
				$.					◯
				$.					◯
				$.					◯
				$.					◯
				$.					◯
				$.					◯
				$.					◯
				$.					◯
				$.					◯
				$.					◯

Date	Payment method	Expense	Category	Amount	Direct debit	Future Fund drawdown	Variable spending	Essential? Y/N	Entered?
				$.					○
				$.					○
				$.					○
				$.					○
				$.					○
				$.					○
				$.					○
				$.					○
				$.					○
				$.					○
				$.					○
				$.					○
				$.					○
				$.					○
				$.					○
				$.					○
				$.					○
				$.					○
				$.					○
				$.					○
				$.					○
				$.					○
				$.					○
				$.					○
				$.					○
				$.					○
				$.					○
				$.					○
				$.					○
				$.					○
				$.					○
				$.					○

Date	Payment method	Expense	Category	Amount	Direct debit	Future Fund drawdown	Variable spending	Essential? Y/N	Entered?
				$.					○
				$.					○
				$.					○
				$.					○
				$.					○
				$.					○
				$.					○
				$.					○
				$.					○
				$.					○
				$.					○
				$.					○
				$.					○
				$.					○
				$.					○
				$.					○
				$.					○
				$.					○
				$.					○
				$.					○
				$.					○
				$.					○
				$.					○
				$.					○
				$.					○
				$.					○
				$.					○
				$.					○
				$.					○
				$.					○
				$.					○
				$.					○
				$.					○

MY NOVEMBER BUDGET SUMMARY

INCOME

	$.		$.
	$.		$.

EXPENSES

Direct debits	Amount	Variable spending	Amount
	$.		$.
	$.		$.
	$.		$.
	$.		$.
	$.		$.
	$.		$.
	$.		$.
	$.		$.
	$.		$.
	$.		$.
Total direct debits	$.		$.
			$.

Future Fund contributions	Amount		
	$.		$.
	$.		$.
	$.		$.
	$.		$.
	$.		$.
	$.		$.
	$.		$.
	$.		$.
	$.		$.
Total Future Fund contributions	$.	**Total variable spending**	$.

		What I will do with this surplus	Amount
TOTAL INCOME	$.		$.
			$.
TOTAL EXPENSES	$.		$.
			$.
AMOUNT LEFT	$.		$.

MY NOVEMBER REFLECTIONS

The three best things that happened to me this month:

....

....

....

The three purchases that brought me the most joy:

....

....

....

My top three achievements at work or study:

....

....

....

The three things I bought that, in hindsight, didn't bring much pleasure:

....

....

....

MONEY MINDMAP CHECK-IN

A negative thought about money I noticed this month was:

....

This thought made me feel: .... (refer to the emotions wheel)

Instead, I choose to flip this thought around and to think that:

....

How I am currently feeling about my money:

MY NOVEMBER CHECKLIST

I am proud to say that this month I successfully (tick as appropriate):

- ☐ Recorded every dollar I spent in my spending tracker
- ☐ Created a monthly summary of my income and expenses
- ☐ Calculated my monthly surplus or deficit
- ☐ If in surplus, I decided how to allocate my surplus funds between paying off debt, increasing my cash buffer or investing and I have completed any transfers of funds or purchases required to implement those decisions
- ☐ If using them, I updated my Future Fund worksheets to reflect my monthly contributions and spending drawdowns
- ☐ Filled out my monthly spending totals on my annual tally sheet on page 210 of this diary
- ☐ Completed this month's Jess' challenge
- ☐ Reminded myself that I am not perfect, but am committed to making small changes to improve my finances

DECEMBER

Be proud of how far you've come

Jess' DECEMBER CHALLENGE

We all need regular opportunities to rest and recharge, and planning ahead can help you to save. Start a fresh Future Fund worksheet to map out your desired holiday expenses for the coming year.

☐ **Challenge accepted**

HABIT TRACKER

○ **Habit 1**

○ **Habit 2**

○ **Habit 3**

○ **Habit 4**

○ **Habit 5**

MONDAY		TUESDAY		WEDNESDAY	

THURSDAY	FRIDAY	SATURDAY	SUNDAY

MY DECEMBER INTENTIONS

The three things I am most looking forward to this month:

....

....

....

My top three priorities at work, study or in family life:

....

....

....

The top three people I want to connect with this month:

....

....

....

The top three events that could prove expensive:

....

....

....

Three fun things I could do this month that are free:

....

....

....

This month will be a success if I can look back and know that:

....

....

....

How I am currently feeling about my money:

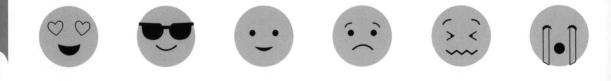

MY DECEMBER SPENDING TRACKER

Date	Payment method	Expense	Category	Amount	Direct debit	Future Fund drawdown	Variable spending	Essential? Y/N	Entered?
				$.					○
				$.					○
				$.					○
				$.					○
				$.					○
				$.					○
				$.					○
				$.					○
				$.					○
				$.					○
				$.					○
				$.					○
				$.					○
				$.					○
				$.					○
				$.					○
				$.					○
				$.					○
				$.					○
				$.					○
				$.					○
				$.					○
				$.					○
				$.					○
				$.					○
				$.					○
				$.					○
				$.					○

Date	Payment method	Expense	Category	Amount	Direct debit	Future Fund drawdown	Variable spending	Essential? Y/N	Entered?
				$.					○
				$.					○
				$.					○
				$.					○
				$.					○
				$.					○
				$.					○
				$.					○
				$.					○
				$.					○
				$.					○
				$.					○
				$.					○
				$.					○
				$.					○
				$.					○
				$.					○
				$.					○
				$.					○
				$.					○
				$.					○
				$.					○
				$.					○
				$.					○
				$.					○
				$.					○
				$.					○
				$.					○
				$.					○
				$.					○
				$.					○
				$.					○

Date	Payment method	Expense	Category	Amount	Direct debit	Future Fund drawdown	Variable spending	Essential? Y/N	Entered?
				$.					○
				$.					○
				$.					○
				$.					○
				$.					○
				$.					○
				$.					○
				$.					○
				$.					○
				$.					○
				$.					○
				$.					○
				$.					○
				$.					○
				$.					○
				$.					○
				$.					○
				$.					○
				$.					○
				$.					○
				$.					○
				$.					○
				$.					○
				$.					○
				$.					○
				$.					○
				$.					○
				$.					○
				$.					○
				$.					○
				$.					○
				$.					○

Date	Payment method	Expense	Category	Amount	Direct debit	Future Fund drawdown	Variable spending	Essential? Y/N	Entered?
				$.					○
				$.					○
				$.					○
				$.					○
				$.					○
				$.					○
				$.					○
				$.					○
				$.					○
				$.					○
				$.					○
				$.					○
				$.					○
				$.					○
				$.					○
				$.					○
				$.					○
				$.					○
				$.					○
				$.					○
				$.					○
				$.					○
				$.					○
				$.					○
				$.					○
				$.					○
				$.					○
				$.					○
				$.					○
				$.					○
				$.					○

Date	Payment method	Expense	Category	Amount	Direct debit	Future Fund drawdown	Variable spending	Essential? Y/N	Entered?
				$.					◯
				$.					◯
				$.					◯
				$.					◯
				$.					◯
				$.					◯
				$.					◯
				$.					◯
				$.					◯
				$.					◯
				$.					◯
				$.					◯
				$.					◯
				$.					◯
				$.					◯
				$.					◯
				$.					◯
				$.					◯
				$.					◯
				$.					◯
				$.					◯
				$.					◯
				$.					◯
				$.					◯
				$.					◯
				$.					◯
				$.					◯
				$.					◯
				$.					◯
				$.					◯
				$.					◯
				$.					◯
				$.					◯
				$.					◯

MY DECEMBER BUDGET SUMMARY

INCOME

	$.		$.
	$.		$.

EXPENSES

Direct debits	Amount	Variable spending	Amount
	$.		$.
	$.		$.
	$.		$.
	$.		$.
	$.		$.
	$.		$.
	$.		$.
	$.		$.
	$.		$.
Total direct debits	$.		$.
			$.

Future Fund contributions	Amount		
	$.		$.
	$.		$.
	$.		$.
	$.		$.
	$.		$.
	$.		$.
	$.		$.
	$.		$.
	$.		$.
Total Future Fund contributions	$.	**Total variable spending**	$.

		What I will do with this surplus	Amount
TOTAL INCOME	$.		$.
			$.
TOTAL EXPENSES	$.		$.
			$.
AMOUNT LEFT	$.		$.

MY DECEMBER REFLECTIONS

The three best things that happened to me this month:

....

....

....

The three purchases that brought me the most joy:

....

....

....

My top three achievements at work or study:

....

....

....

The three things I bought that, in hindsight, didn't bring much pleasure:

....

....

....

MONEY MINDMAP CHECK-IN

A negative thought about money I noticed this month was:

....

This thought made me feel: .... (refer to the emotions wheel)

Instead, I choose to flip this thought around and to think that:

....

How I am currently feeling about my money:

MY DECEMBER CHECKLIST

I am proud to say that this month I successfully (tick as appropriate):

- ☐ Recorded every dollar I spent in my spending tracker

- ☐ Created a monthly summary of my income and expenses

- ☐ Calculated my monthly surplus or deficit

- ☐ If in surplus, I decided how to allocate my surplus funds between paying off debt, increasing my cash buffer or investing and I have completed any transfers of funds or purchases required to implement those decisions

- ☐ If using them, I updated my Future Fund worksheets to reflect my monthly contributions and spending drawdowns

- ☐ Filled out my monthly spending totals on my annual tally sheet on page 210 of this diary

- ☐ Completed this month's Jess' challenge

- ☐ Reminded myself that I am not perfect, but am committed to making small changes to improve my finances

PART THREE

REFLECT

CHAPTER 9

YOUR MONEY
YEAR IN REVIEW

Congratulations! You've made it through a full year of tracking your spending. What insights have you gained?

It's now time to take all the information you've gathered across the year and distil it. We'll spot the trends and patterns and create a complete picture of where your money actually goes.

In this final part of the book, we'll tally your annual expenses. After that, we'll create a highlights reel of your year and look for clues as to what these reveal about your true life values. We'll also check in again on your level of financial wellbeing and fill in another money snapshot to see how your debts and assets have changed over the year.

Finally, I'll provide you with my best tips and tricks for where to go next on your journey towards not only sustaining a more constructive and healthy attitude towards managing your money, but also building your wealth for the longer term.

There was a time when, if you had asked me to tell you my annual spending, you would have just received a blank stare in response. On the inside, I would have been thinking what an outlandishly complex and ridiculous question this was and how nobody—absolutely nobody—could be expected to know the answer to it. But guess what? Today I know pretty much exactly what my annual living expenses are. And because you've stuck with me for so long on this journey, you're about to too.

I think that's a wonderful achievement that you should feel very proud of. And it will help you in myriad ways. You see, society expects you to already know this information. When you apply for a loan, you will be asked to state your monthly living expenses. As you save up for retirement, you'll be asked what income you need in order to sustain your annual living costs. And even sooner than that, most financial gurus will blithely advise you to have between three and six months' worth of living expenses saved up in an emergency fund.

A less obvious perk of knowing your annual living expenses is that, once you do, you can tailor your working life to them. Remember, while some of you are perhaps out there working for the pure pleasure of it (really?), most of us are out there working to generate the income we need to fund our lifetime needs and wants.

Once you know what these needs and wants are—and how much they cost—you can work backwards to figure out how much you actually need to work. Perhaps you realise you are under-earning and you really need to push more aggressively for that pay rise, or to consider an alternative employer or career. Perhaps, if you're doing well with your work and career but your personal life is shot, you can use your knowledge of your living expenses to plan a career pause, to scale back your hours, or even to achieve that holy grail of early retirement.

So whether it's being able to borrow with more confidence, plan for retirement, sleep well at night with an adequate emergency buffer or leave a job you don't enjoy, I hope you agree with me that the exercise we're about to do is worthwhile indeed. Let's get started!

Your annual spending review

Starting with January, flick back to your monthly budget summaries and fill in your expenses for each line in the 'My annual spending review' table that you'll find over the next few pages.

Methodically go through each category and subcategory and pull out your monthly total for each one. Take your time with this and enjoy the ride. As you start to fill in all the blanks on the following pages (just put a dash or straight line through any with no expenses), you'll start to see the fluctuating trends in your spending over time. Relish it. Notice your internal reactions to months where expenses have been well above or below other months. Did that higher spending bring you joy? Or would you like to double down on minimising expenses in that area?

If you used Future Funds to cover some of your spending, you'll need to check your drawdowns from these (these are not shown on your monthly summary sheets). So remember to go through those too and group expenses into their relevant subcategory and include them in the table. As I say, do pace yourself. Work methodically.

It's entirely possible you'll find gaps in what you've tracked. Just do your best. Feel free to white out any categories you didn't use and add your own. Extra points if you highlight your completed rows with your highlighter colour corresponding to that category. ☺

Keep sight of the overarching goal, which is to come up with an estimate of your annual living expenses. I've been doing this for a number of years, and it is possible. But if this is all still a bit new and you're unsure of a number, it's okay to put in your best estimate. It's all a learning experience and you can always try again next year!

Over to you … I hope you enjoy doing this. ☺

MY ANNUAL SPENDING REVIEW

Category	Subcategory	Jan	Feb	Mar	Apr	May
HOUSING	Rent / mortgage	$.	$.	$.	$.	$.
HOUSEHOLD	Furniture	$.	$.	$.	$.	$.
	Décor	$.	$.	$.	$.	$.
	Appliances	$.	$.	$.	$.	$.
	Home maintenance and repairs	$.	$.	$.	$.	$.
	Cleaning	$.	$.	$.	$.	$.
	Hygiene	$.	$.	$.	$.	$.
	Garden	$.	$.	$.	$.	$.
	Strata fees	$.	$.	$.	$.	$.
	Home insurance	$.	$.	$.	$.	$.
	Council rates	$.	$.	$.	$.	$.
	Household services	$.	$.	$.	$.	$.
	TOTAL	$.	$.	$.	$.	$.
UTILITIES	Electricity	$.	$.	$.	$.	$.
	Gas	$.	$.	$.	$.	$.
	Water and sewerage	$.	$.	$.	$.	$.
	Internet	$.	$.	$.	$.	$.
	Phone	$.	$.	$.	$.	$.
	Postal services	$.	$.	$.	$.	$.
	TOTAL	$.	$.	$.	$.	$.
TRANSPORT	Vehicle purchase	$.	$.	$.	$.	$.
	Vehicle loan payments	$.	$.	$.	$.	$.
	Vehicle registration	$.	$.	$.	$.	$.
	Drivers licence	$.	$.	$.	$.	$.
	Vehicle insurance	$.	$.	$.	$.	$.
	Vehicle servicing and repairs	$.	$.	$.	$.	$.
	Vehicle parts and accessories	$.	$.	$.	$.	$.
	Roadside assist	$.	$.	$.	$.	$.
	Driving lessons	$.	$.	$.	$.	$.
	Fuel	$.	$.	$.	$.	$.
	Tolls	$.	$.	$.	$.	$.

June	July	Aug	Sept	Oct	Nov	Dec	Total
$.	$.	$.	$.	$.	$.	$.	$.
$.	$.	$.	$.	$.	$.	$.	$.
$.	$.	$.	$.	$.	$.	$.	$.
$.	$.	$.	$.	$.	$.	$.	$.
$.	$.	$.	$.	$.	$.	$.	$.
$.	$.	$.	$.	$.	$.	$.	$.
$.	$.	$.	$.	$.	$.	$.	$.
$.	$.	$.	$.	$.	$.	$.	$.
$.	$.	$.	$.	$.	$.	$.	$.
$.	$.	$.	$.	$.	$.	$.	$.
$.	$.	$.	$.	$.	$.	$.	$.
$.	$.	$.	$.	$.	$.	$.	$.
$.	$.	$.	$.	$.	$.	$.	$.
$.	$.	$.	$.	$.	$.	$.	$.
$.	$.	$.	$.	$.	$.	$.	$.
$.	$.	$.	$.	$.	$.	$.	$.
$.	$.	$.	$.	$.	$.	$.	$.
$.	$.	$.	$.	$.	$.	$.	$.
$.	$.	$.	$.	$.	$.	$.	$.
$.	$.	$.	$.	$.	$.	$.	$.
$.	$.	$.	$.	$.	$.	$.	$.
$.	$.	$.	$.	$.	$.	$.	$.
$.	$.	$.	$.	$.	$.	$.	$.
$.	$.	$.	$.	$.	$.	$.	$.
$.	$.	$.	$.	$.	$.	$.	$.
$.	$.	$.	$.	$.	$.	$.	$.
$.	$.	$.	$.	$.	$.	$.	$.
$.	$.	$.	$.	$.	$.	$.	$.
$.	$.	$.	$.	$.	$.	$.	$.
$.	$.	$.	$.	$.	$.	$.	$.

Category	Subcategory	Jan	Feb	Mar	Apr	May
	Parking	$.	$.	$.	$.	$.
	Public transport	$.	$.	$.	$.	$.
	Vehicle hire, taxi and ride shares	$.	$.	$.	$.	$.
	TOTAL	$.	$.	$.	$.	$.
FOOD		$.	$.	$.	$.	$.
HEALTH	Health insurance	$.	$.	$.	$.	$.
	Pet insurance and veterinary costs	$.	$.	$.	$.	$.
	Doctors and specialists	$.	$.	$.	$.	$.
	Dental	$.	$.	$.	$.	$.
	Optical	$.	$.	$.	$.	$.
	Hospital and ambulance	$.	$.	$.	$.	$.
	Medicines	$.	$.	$.	$.	$.
	Medical equipment	$.	$.	$.	$.	$.
	Sport and fitness	$.	$.	$.	$.	$.
	TOTAL	$.	$.	$.	$.	$.
EDUCATION	Books, newspapers and magazines	$.	$.	$.	$.	$.
	Stationery	$.	$.	$.	$.	$.
	Home computer equipment	$.	$.	$.	$.	$.
	Childcare	$.	$.	$.	$.	$.
	School	$.	$.	$.	$.	$.
	Higher education	$.	$.	$.	$.	$.
	TOTAL	$.	$.	$.	$.	$.
APPEARANCE	Clothes and shoes	$.	$.	$.	$.	$.
	Accessories	$.	$.	$.	$.	$.
	Hairdressing	$.	$.	$.	$.	$.
	Beauty products	$.	$.	$.	$.	$.
	Beauty treatments	$.	$.	$.	$.	$.
	TOTAL	$.	$.	$.	$.	$.

June	July	Aug	Sept	Oct	Nov	Dec	Total
$.	$.	$.	$.	$.	$.	$.	$.
$.	$.	$.	$.	$.	$.	$.	$.
$.	$.	$.	$.	$.	$.	$.	$.
$.	$.	$.	$.	$.	$.	$.	$.
$.	$.	$.	$.	$.	$.	$.	$.
$.	$.	$.	$.	$.	$.	$.	$.
$.	$.	$.	$.	$.	$.	$.	$.
$.	$.	$.	$.	$.	$.	$.	$.
$.	$.	$.	$.	$.	$.	$.	$.
$.	$.	$.	$.	$.	$.	$.	$.
$.	$.	$.	$.	$.	$.	$.	$.
$.	$.	$.	$.	$.	$.	$.	$.
$.	$.	$.	$.	$.	$.	$.	$.
$.	$.	$.	$.	$.	$.	$.	$.
$.	$.	$.	$.	$.	$.	$.	$.
$.	$.	$.	$.	$.	$.	$.	$.
$.	$.	$.	$.	$.	$.	$.	$.
$.	$.	$.	$.	$.	$.	$.	$.
$.	$.	$.	$.	$.	$.	$.	$.
$.	$.	$.	$.	$.	$.	$.	$.
$.	$.	$.	$.	$.	$.	$.	$.
$.	$.	$.	$.	$.	$.	$.	$.
$.	$.	$.	$.	$.	$.	$.	$.
$.	$.	$.	$.	$.	$.	$.	$.
$.	$.	$.	$.	$.	$.	$.	$.
$.	$.	$.	$.	$.	$.	$.	$.
$.	$.	$.	$.	$.	$.	$.	$.

Category	Subcategory	Jan	Feb	Mar	Apr	May
LIFESTYLE	Eating out and takeaway	$.	$.	$.	$.	$.
	Alcohol	$.	$.	$.	$.	$.
	Tobacco & drugs	$.	$.	$.	$.	$.
	Holidays	$.	$.	$.	$.	$.
	Seasonal celebrations	$.	$.	$.	$.	$.
	Parties and functions	$.	$.	$.	$.	$.
	Gifts	$.	$.	$.	$.	$.
	Toys	$.	$.	$.	$.	$.
	Streaming services	$.	$.	$.	$.	$.
	Gaming and consoles	$.	$.	$.	$.	$.
	Music, audio and photographic	$.	$.	$.	$.	$.
	Live entertainment	$.	$.	$.	$.	$.
	Attractions	$.	$.	$.	$.	$.
	Hobbies	$.	$.	$.	$.	$.
	Gambling	$.	$.	$.	$.	$.
	Pet purchases	$.	$.	$.	$.	$.
	TOTAL	$.	$.	$.	$.	$.
PROFESSIONAL FEES	Credit cards	$.	$.	$.	$.	$.
	Other loans	$.	$.	$.	$.	$.
	Bank fees	$.	$.	$.	$.	$.
	Life / trauma / TPD insurance	$.	$.	$.	$.	$.
	Income protection insurance	$.	$.	$.	$.	$.
	Financial advisor fees	$.	$.	$.	$.	$.
	Accountant / tax agent fees	$.	$.	$.	$.	$.
	Legal fees	$.	$.	$.	$.	$.
	Funeral expenses	$.	$.	$.	$.	$.
	Union / professional association fees	$.	$.	$.	$.	$.
	Child support	$.	$.	$.	$.	$.
	Pocket money	$.	$.	$.	$.	$.
	Charity donations	$.	$.	$.	$.	$.
	TOTAL	$.	$.	$.	$.	$.
TOTAL ALL CATEGORIES		$.	$.	$.	$.	$.

June	July	Aug	Sept	Oct	Nov	Dec	Total
$.	$.	$.	$.	$.	$.	$.	$.
$.	$.	$.	$.	$.	$.	$.	$.
$.	$.	$.	$.	$.	$.	$.	$.
$.	$.	$.	$.	$.	$.	$.	$.
$.	$.	$.	$.	$.	$.	$.	$.
$.	$.	$.	$.	$.	$.	$.	$.
$.	$.	$.	$.	$.	$.	$.	$.
$.	$.	$.	$.	$.	$.	$.	$.
$.	$.	$.	$.	$.	$.	$.	$.
$.	$.	$.	$.	$.	$.	$.	$.
$.	$.	$.	$.	$.	$.	$.	$.
$.	$.	$.	$.	$.	$.	$.	$.
$.	$.	$.	$.	$.	$.	$.	$.
$.	$.	$.	$.	$.	$.	$.	$.
$.	$.	$.	$.	$.	$.	$.	$.
$.	$.	$.	$.	$.	$.	$.	$.
$.	$.	$.	$.	$.	$.	$.	$.
$.	$.	$.	$.	$.	$.	$.	$.
$.	$.	$.	$.	$.	$.	$.	$.
$.	$.	$.	$.	$.	$.	$.	$.
$.	$.	$.	$.	$.	$.	$.	$.
$.	$.	$.	$.	$.	$.	$.	$.
$.	$.	$.	$.	$.	$.	$.	$.
$.	$.	$.	$.	$.	$.	$.	$.
$.	$.	$.	$.	$.	$.	$.	$.
$.	$.	$.	$.	$.	$.	$.	$.
$.	$.	$.	$.	$.	$.	$.	$.

CHAPTER 10

REFLECT ON YOUR GREATEST HITS THIS YEAR

I'd like you to now look back over the year that was and your monthly reflections to come up with three 'Top 10 hits' lists for the year gone by.

First we'll consider your Top 10 favourite purchases for the year. You can do this by reviewing your top three purchases for each month, as recorded in your monthly reflections. Rank your top purchases from 1 to 10.

Hopefully this process will fill you with a sense of joy and gratitude about the wonderful ways you've allocated your money throughout the year. Perhaps the types of purchases you enjoyed changed over the year, pointing to an evolution in what brings you pleasure.

Next, we'll create a Top 10 list of your absolute favourite moments throughout the year, also as recorded in your monthly reflections. What were the best things that happened to you?

In both exercises, we'll be looking for underlying patterns to help point you in the direction of your top life values. Knowing what you value in life can be such a helpful guide to inform your future spending and create the life you truly desire.

If you love spending money on travel, for example, one of your life values might be 'freedom'. If you love purchasing gifts for friends or family, one of your highest values might be 'connection'.

Finally, create a Top 10 list of your greatest work achievements this year — don't forget to show it to your boss!

I hope you enjoy this opportunity to pause and reflect on what brought you joy this year.

MY TOP 10 PURCHASES

What were the 10 purchases that brought you the most joy? Which categories did they fall into, and what do you think this says about what you truly value in life? Spend some time reflecting on this and write your list below.

For example, one purchase might have been return flights to Bali, cost $1000, category: 'holidays', what you enjoyed most: spending time with friends and relaxing, life value: 'fun'.

	Purchase	Cost	Category	What did you enjoy most about this?	Which life value do you think this best represents? (see list on page 31)
1		$.			
2		$.			
3		$.			
4		$.			
5		$.			
6		$.			
7		$.			
8		$.			
9		$.			
10		$.			

MY TOP 10 BEST THINGS THAT HAPPENED

Look back over your monthly reflection sheets again and create a personal highlights reel for the year. It's so easy to get lost in the day to day, and forget all the fun stuff we've done throughout the year, be it spending time in nature, or with friends, or celebrating big career or life milestones.

So, pick the eyes out of your monthly 'best things that happened to me' lists (from your monthly reflections worksheets in chapter 8) and write your 'Top 10' below. Reflect on what has been important to you and what life values these things reflect.

	Event	What in particular did you enjoy about this?	Which life value does this best represent?
1			
2			
3			
4			
5			
6			
7			
8			
9			
10			

MY TOP 10 ACHIEVEMENTS AT WORK

You really are the most powerful income-generating asset you own. It's time to celebrate all your work wins this year and reflect on the values you have demonstrated, such as courage, creativity and care.

For those of you in paid employment, now is the time to look back and create a 'greatest hits' list of your work achievements.

Don't hide your light under a bushel ... make sure your boss knows about all these great achievements too!

	Work achievement	Life value this demonstrated
1		
2		
3		
4		
5		
6		
7		
8		
9		
10		

CHAPTER 11:

TAKE YOUR MONEY 'AFTER' SNAPSHOT

Now, do you remember when we smiled and said 'cheese' for your money 'before' snapshot in chapter 3? It's time to revisit that to see how far you've come.

The only way to really grow your total wealth in the long run (sparing having rich parents or winning the lottery) is to consistently spend less than you earn to generate savings that can be invested.

Hopefully, you're more in touch than you used to be on whether this has been the case throughout the year. You'll have calculated your monthly surpluses or deficits, and also collated your annual estimate of the same.

So hopefully there will be no surprises when you come to see if you've managed to increase or decrease your net worth during the year.

Of course, returns on any investments you have — improvements or decreases in the value of your property and super — will have made an impact.

Remember, as much as we're trying to get you more in control of managing your money, life will always throw you its curveballs. So if you have not seen much improvement in your net worth this year, don't worry. At least now you know.

And if you have managed to grow your wealth, that's great too — big pats on the back to you.

And remember, there's always next year.

Another way to measure your potential progress is not in dollars and cents, but in how you *feel* about your money. Before you fill in your money 'after' snapshot (see page 220), have a go at repeating the financial wellbeing questionnaire from the introduction to this book. You'll find a copy of it on the next page just for that purpose ... go on: see how far you've come!

FINANCIAL WELLBEING QUESTIONNAIRE

If you'd like to test your current level of financial wellbeing, researchers at Australia's The Melbourne Institute and the Commonwealth Bank designed the following simple test to help. Simply work your way through it and circle a response for each part. Don't overthink it – go with your gut.

How well do the following statements describe you or your situation?

I can enjoy life because of the way I'm managing my money

☐ Not at all   ☐ Very little   ☐ Somewhat   ☐ Very well   ☐ Completely

I could handle a major unexpected expense

☐ Not at all   ☐ Very little   ☐ Somewhat   ☐ Very well   ☐ Completely

When it comes to how you think and feel about your finances, please indicate the extent to which you agree or disagree with the following statements.

I feel on top of my day-to-day finances

☐ Disagree strongly   ☐ Disagree   ☐ Neither agree nor disagree   ☐ Agree   ☐ Agree strongly

I am comfortable with my current levels of spending relative to the funds I have coming in

☐ Disagree strongly   ☐ Disagree   ☐ Neither agree nor disagree   ☐ Agree   ☐ Agree strongly

I am on track to have enough money to provide for my financial needs in the future

☐ Disagree strongly   ☐ Disagree   ☐ Neither agree nor disagree   ☐ Agree   ☐ Agree strongly

Now, for each question answered, give yourself a score of between 0 and 4. Give a score of 4 for each statement you answered 'Completely' or 'Agree strongly' with, 3 for each 'Very well' or 'Agree', 2 for each 'Somewhat' or 'Neither agree nor disagree', 1 for each 'Very little' or 'Disagree' and 0 for each 'Not at all' or 'Disagree strongly'.

Add up your total score and multiply it by 5 to get a score out of 100.

MY SCORE: ....

MY PREVIOUS SCORE: ....

MY MONEY 'AFTER' SNAPSHOT

Return to your money 'before' snapshot from chapter 3 and update your estimates for the values of what you own versus what you owe. Of course, add in any extra debts or assets you have acquired over the past 12 months.

Date: ....

WHAT I OWN...

Asset	Estimated value
	$
	$
	$
	$
	$
	$
	$
TOTAL	$

WHAT I OWE...

Liability	Amount
	$
	$
	$
	$
	$
	$
	$
TOTAL	$

MY NET WORTH

What I own minus what I owe: $ ....

WHERE TO NOW?

So, how are you feeling? We've just performed rather a lot of maths and analytics to get you to the numbers you need to take control of your money life.

I realise that maths was not everyone's favourite subject in school, and that this might have been quite a big ask for many of you. It's time to connect all those numbers back to what we really came here for.

We started this diary with the intention of lessening your worries when it comes to your money. We came to work on your relationship with money through honesty and openness.

Have a look back at what you wrote at the start of the year on page 16 about how you were thinking and feeling about money. Do you feel that way now?

As much as I believe we can shift and improve our feelings around certain topics, I also know it's not a 180-degree thing. If you've started out a bit overwhelmed and scared of money, I'd actually be surprised if you're ending the year feeing completely the opposite emotions of hope and optimism 100 per cent of the time.

I still have periods of time when I worry a bit more about money—that's natural.

I still have times when life gets crazy and I'm overwhelmed and don't want to engage with it. But I also know to take opposite action. And in those times, if I return to my money tracking and diarising, it calms me and gives me greater peace of mind.

I have accepted that confronting my own fears and insecurities around money will be a lifetime thing. You can't change your lifetime's thoughts and emotions around money in one year.

You can, however, remain committed to doing the work and taking the time to engage with your hard-earned money and make sure you are in control of where it's going.

So what's next? I would advocate more of the same. Yes, sometimes some of the biggest insights gained from tracking your spending come in the first weeks and months. But I also think they compound.

Tracking my spending and tallying my monthly budget is just part of the rhythm of my life these days. It's as habitual and ordinary to me as brushing my teeth or having a shower. If I don't keep doing it, it just feels a bit wrong.

I absolutely know in my bones that my life is happier and I can make better decisions when I continue to pay close attention to my money and where it is going.

There are those who advise that money management is like planting a tree. You get your system of automation in place and you walk away. There are those who would poke fun at or diminish someone who is so diligent in tracking their spending. And I guess there are those who are so comfortably well off, that it simply becomes unnecessary.

If you fall into any of those camps and it works for you, I have no beef with that.

If tracking your spending is an experiment you've tried simply to see what it's like but you'd really rather be doing something else with your time, I can't stop you. And I wouldn't want to.

Because if there is a philosophy underpinning this whole exercise, it's this: You do you.

You spend your money how *you* want to. You spend your time how *you* want to. Manage your money how *you* want to.

Just give it a bit of thought, okay? Make sure you're not spending your money the way society expects you to, or your parents expect you to, or your school friends expect you to. If you get only one thing out of this diary and this experience I hope it's to keep questioning your decisions—yes, mostly about money, but also about life.

Do your actions—spending, or otherwise—match your values? Are you making time for the things that truly bring *you* pleasure?

That's what it's really all about.

As for me, I intend to keep tracking my spending each year, using this cool new diary I've made (selfish, remember?) and I hope you'll join me too.

Continuing to track my spending keeps me in the driver's seat of where my money is going, even when life wants to blow me off course.

I look after my money and pay close attention to it in the way I've just shown you because this process in itself brings me joy.

When I write in my spending tracker, it's like writing a little love note to myself. I love and honour my money because I love and honour myself.

I honour the time I've spent working to earn the money I have coming into my life. And I value myself enough to care that I am living — and spending — in alignment with my values and what brings me true pleasure.

I love and pay attention to my money like 12-year-old Jess loved and studied the wave of Luke Perry's hair, the curve of his pursed lips, the piercing gaze of his stare. It's the little details that make up the whole effect.

If there is a polar opposite to the emotion of fear, it must be love. And it is the emotion of 'love' that I would most dearly like you to experience with your money. Fear drives us away from something, but love pulls us closer.

I love my money. I'm proud of it. I take care of it. When I'm sloppy with it and spend it on things that are not in alignment with my values, I feel bad. And this drives me to do better.

And in return, my money loves me back. When I look after and build my money, it protects me. It frees me. And it brings me pleasure in so many ways.

I'd like for you to love your money because I know the protection it can bring. But mostly I want you to love and nurture your money because I want you to love and nurture yourself. Respect the hours of your life you gave up to earn your dollars and mindfully spend your hard-earned money in ways that bring you true joy.

So, love your money and love your life. But most of all, love yourself.

Because I know you're worth it.

Take care,

Jess xx

NOTES